Ancient History's Connection To Religious Evolution

Dedication

This book is dedicated to the tireless seekers of truth, those who dare to question, to compare, and to connect the disparate threads of human experience. It is dedicated to the scholars past and present who have dedicated their lives to illuminating the rich tapestry of ancient religious traditions, tirelessly deciphering texts and interpreting symbols, illuminating the shared humanity woven into the fabric of diverse beliefs. This work is also a tribute to the enduring power of storytelling, the way narratives – whether enshrined in epic poems, sacred scriptures, or whispered myths – have shaped civilizations, instilled values, and offered solace and meaning across millennia. Finally, this is dedicated to the curiosity that drives us to look beyond the surface, to find common ground amidst apparent differences, and to glimpse the universal human longing for understanding and connection, a longing echoed across time and across cultures. May this exploration inspire further investigation and deeper understanding of the rich spiritual heritage of our shared past.

Preface

The undertaking of this comparative study of ancient religious traditions has been an intellectually enriching and deeply humbling experience. Initially, the sheer diversity of belief systems – from the polytheistic pantheons of ancient Greece and Egypt to the monotheistic faiths of the Abrahamic traditions and the philosophical depth of Buddhism – seemed daunting. However, as I delved into the texts, a remarkable pattern emerged: a surprising convergence of themes, archetypes, and moral messages despite vast geographical and chronological differences. This book is not intended to impose a single, unifying narrative onto these diverse traditions; rather, it aims to highlight the striking parallels that exist, recognizing the crucial importance of historical and cultural context. The careful consideration of these contexts is paramount, as is acknowledging the inherent limitations of any comparative study. Nevertheless, the commonalities identified – such as the recurrence of flood myths, hero's journeys, creation accounts, and afterlife beliefs – point towards fundamental aspects of the human condition, a shared yearning for understanding our place in the universe and finding meaning in a world often characterized by suffering and uncertainty. The process of writing this book has been one of continuous learning, discovery, and a profound appreciation for the enduring human quest for spiritual and ethical guidance. I hope that this exploration will resonate with readers and inspire further inquiry into the timeless wisdom embedded within these ancient texts.

Introduction

This book embarks on a journey through the rich tapestry of ancient religious traditions, seeking to uncover surprising parallels and common threads woven into their narratives. By examining a diverse range of texts – from the Epic of Gilgamesh and the Sumerian creation myths to the Book of the Dead, the Ten Commandments, the Kybalion, the Bible, the Quran, and the Torah – we aim to demonstrate that despite significant geographical and temporal differences, these ancient faiths share remarkable similarities in core beliefs and storylines. Our analysis extends beyond the most well-known texts, venturing into apocryphal writings and lesser-known traditions to enrich the comparative study. This broad approach allows us to identify recurring themes and archetypes, such as the ubiquitous flood myths, the archetypal hero's journey, the recurring concepts of creation and destruction, and the persistent human fascination with the afterlife. The book is structured thematically, enabling readers to readily trace these recurring themes across vastly different cultures and time periods. This thematic approach facilitates clear comparisons, highlighting both the similarities and the significant differences in how these themes are expressed and understood within each tradition. Crucially, we recognize and acknowledge the importance of contextualizing each belief system within its specific historical and cultural setting. The book does not seek to impose a single, overarching interpretation but rather to facilitate a deeper understanding and appreciation for the intricate interplay of shared human experiences and unique cultural expressions. Ultimately, this comparative study suggests that these shared narratives are not merely coincidences but reflections of fundamental aspects of the human condition – the enduring search for meaning, purpose, and understanding in a world characterized by both wonder and suffering.

Defining Comparative Religion and its Methodology

Comparative religion, at its core, is the systematic study of religious traditions across cultures and historical periods. It's a discipline that transcends the limitations of studying individual faiths in isolation, instead seeking to identify commonalities, differences, and patterns within the diverse tapestry of human religious expression. Unlike the approach of a theologian focused on the internal consistency and development of a single faith, comparative religion embraces a broader perspective, employing methodologies designed to uncover both the unique characteristics and shared elements of various belief systems. This necessitates a critical and nuanced approach, acknowledging the inherent complexities of interpreting ancient texts within their specific historical and cultural contexts.

The methodology of comparative religion involves a multifaceted approach. It begins with the careful selection of texts and traditions for comparative analysis. This selection process should reflect a commitment to inclusivity and representativeness, avoiding biases toward dominant or widely studied religions. The choice of texts will depend on the specific focus of the research, but it often involves primary source materials like sacred scriptures, mythological narratives, religious rituals, and philosophical treatises. The analysis then moves to a systematic comparison, identifying common themes, motifs, and narratives across different traditions. This involves meticulously documenting similarities and differences in beliefs, practices, and values. The act of comparison, however, should not be a superficial exercise in finding superficial similarities; rather, it should be driven by a clear research question or hypothesis. For example, one might compare the concept of divine judgment in ancient Egyptian religion, with the Judeo-Christian concept of the Last Judgment or the Buddhist concept of Karma and rebirth. What are the similarities and differences? What does comparing these reveal about common anxieties, beliefs and worldviews concerning the afterlife?

Crucially, comparative religion emphasizes the importance of contextualization. Each religious tradition must be understood within its unique historical, cultural, and geographical setting. This means considering factors such as the social structures, political climate, economic conditions, and environmental influences that have shaped the development of a particular religious belief system. Ignoring context risks misinterpreting symbols, rituals, and narratives, leading to erroneous conclusions. For instance, the depiction of gods and goddesses in ancient polytheistic religions should not be evaluated through the lens of modern monotheistic frameworks. Understanding the social roles and functions of these deities within their respective societies is crucial for accurate interpretation. Similarly, the interpretation of sacred texts requires an awareness of the historical processes involved in their creation, transmission, and redaction. Texts are not static entities; they evolve over time, often undergoing changes in interpretation and adaptation to new contexts.

This book takes a comparative approach, examining five major ancient religious traditions: Greek, Roman, Egyptian, Buddhist, and Abrahamic (Judaism, Christianity, and Islam). Each tradition will be considered on its own merits, respecting its unique features. The analysis, however, moves beyond simple description, identifying common themes and shared patterns while also acknowledging significant differences. The core methodologies guiding the analysis include careful textual analysis, comparative mythology, anthropological analysis of religious practices, and historical contextualization. This allows for a rigorous and nuanced comparison, avoiding simplistic generalizations and emphasizing the complexity of religious beliefs and practices.

Within this framework, we will examine a selection of key texts representing these traditions. The Epic of Gilgamesh, from ancient Mesopotamia, offers a rich tapestry of myths, legends, and reflections on human life, including a powerful flood narrative that finds parallels in other traditions. The Book of the Dead, a collection of ancient Egyptian funerary texts, reveals intricate beliefs about the afterlife, judgment, and the journey of the soul. The Abrahamic traditions – Judaism, Christianity, and Islam – will be explored through their foundational texts: the Torah, the Bible (including the Old and New Testaments), and the Quran. These texts provide a vast range of narratives, moral codes, and theological insights that allow for illuminating comparisons across cultures and time. Furthermore, we will also examine Buddhist scriptures, which detail the life of the Buddha, the concept of karma and rebirth, and the path to enlightenment. These varied texts will serve as primary sources for our comparative analysis, allowing us to explore the shared concerns and diverse expressions of ancient religious thought.

One of the key advantages of employing a comparative approach is its potential to expose underlying patterns and universal themes that might otherwise remain obscured. By systematically analyzing different traditions, we can gain a more comprehensive understanding of the human condition and the enduring search for meaning and purpose. This approach helps us avoid ethnocentric biases, recognizing that human beings across different cultures and time periods have grappled with similar existential questions: the nature of reality, the meaning of life and death, the nature of good and evil, and the relationship between humanity and the divine or supernatural.

The limitations of comparative religion should also be acknowledged. Directly comparing disparate cultures and belief systems is fraught with potential pitfalls. Translating ancient texts, and interpreting their meaning, involves inherent complexities. Linguistic nuances, cultural assumptions, and the limitations of our own understanding can lead to misinterpretations. Moreover, the very act of comparison risks imposing a framework on ancient beliefs and practices that might not be entirely appropriate. Ancient cultures had their own systems of thought and categorization, which may not map neatly onto our modern ways of understanding the world. It's crucial, therefore, to approach these texts with humility and respect, avoiding imposing modern perspectives and acknowledging the limits of our knowledge. This book will strive to minimize these potential pitfalls by paying close attention to the specific historical and cultural contexts of each tradition and by engaging with diverse scholarly interpretations.

Despite these challenges, the benefits of comparative religious studies are substantial. By identifying shared patterns and universal themes, we gain a broader and deeper understanding of humanity's religious impulse, its capacity for spiritual expression, and its ongoing struggle with fundamental existential questions. The exploration of ancient religious traditions is not a mere academic exercise; it offers valuable insights into the enduring human search for meaning and purpose, insights that remain relevant even in our contemporary world. The shared narratives, beliefs and practices across vastly different cultures and timelines reveal something fundamental about the human condition; our persistent quest to understand ourselves, our place in the universe, and the larger purpose of existence. The parallels between different mythologies, ethical systems and afterlife beliefs offer powerful and compelling evidence for the deeply rooted human need for such meaning. This study allows us to examine and ponder the nature of these enduring questions and the creative ways that different societies have responded to them throughout history.

The following chapters will delve into specific thematic areas, providing detailed comparative analyses of creation myths, flood narratives, afterlife beliefs, hero myths, moral codes, and the roles of divine figures. We will explore both major and lesser-known traditions, including apocryphal texts and other less-studied materials, to offer a richer and more nuanced understanding of the complexities of ancient religious thought. Through this examination, we aim to illuminate the remarkable parallels and enduring relevance of ancient spiritual and ethical wisdom. This study provides a framework for understanding the universality of human spiritual experiences and their enduring power to inspire, console, and guide humanity in its ongoing search for meaning.

The Scope and Limitations of Comparative Religious Studies

The endeavor to compare religious systems across vastly different cultures and historical epochs, while offering profound insights into the human condition, is not without its inherent limitations and challenges. The very act of comparison necessitates a critical awareness of the potential pitfalls, ensuring that the analysis remains rigorous and avoids simplistic generalizations that might misrepresent the nuanced complexities of ancient beliefs and practices.

One major hurdle lies in the inherent biases that can inadvertently shape the comparative process. Researchers, often unconsciously, may favor perspectives or traditions more familiar to them, leading to skewed interpretations. This can manifest in several ways. For instance, the selection of texts for comparison might unintentionally privilege those from more dominant or well-studied religious traditions, neglecting lesser-known or marginalized faiths. This selective bias can result in an incomplete and potentially inaccurate representation of the wider landscape of religious expression. Moreover, the researcher's own cultural background and worldview can subtly influence the interpretation of ancient texts and practices. Implicit biases, stemming from upbringing, education, and personal beliefs, might inadvertently shape the way in which similarities and differences are identified and evaluated.

Further complicating the comparative process are the difficulties in translating and interpreting ancient texts. The sheer linguistic diversity across different cultures and historical periods presents a significant challenge. Even with the aid of expert translations, subtle nuances in meaning can be lost, potentially leading to misinterpretations of core religious concepts and beliefs. Moreover, the process of translation often involves choices and interpretations that can subtly alter the meaning of the original text. Words, phrases, and metaphors that might have held specific cultural or religious significance in their original context may not have direct equivalents in modern languages. This inherent ambiguity can introduce uncertainties into the comparative analysis, requiring researchers to exercise extreme caution and carefully acknowledge the limitations of any given translation.

Furthermore, the act of comparison itself can be problematic. By attempting to align vastly different religious systems within a single framework, we risk imposing a structure or interpretive lens that might not accurately reflect the original context. Ancient cultures possessed unique ways of organizing knowledge, categorizing experience, and expressing religious beliefs. These systems of thought may not neatly align with our modern categories and conceptual frameworks. For example, comparing the concept of "God" across monotheistic and polytheistic traditions requires a careful understanding of the diverse meanings and functions associated with the divine in different cultural contexts. Simple equivalences can obscure profound differences in religious understanding. Similarly, attempts to compare ritual practices across diverse cultures necessitate a nuanced understanding of the specific social, political, and economic circumstances within which these practices were embedded.

The historical context of the texts and traditions being compared is also crucial. Religious systems evolve over time, responding to changing social, political, and environmental conditions. A comparative analysis must consider the historical development of each tradition, taking into account the diverse factors that have shaped its beliefs and practices. Comparing a mature, codified religious system with an earlier, less developed one necessitates a careful consideration of the evolutionary processes that led to its current form. Moreover, comparing a religious tradition in one geographic region with a similar tradition in another requires an understanding of the different cultural influences and interactions that might have shaped its unique features.

Another crucial limitation is the nature of surviving evidence. Many ancient religious practices and beliefs are only known to us through fragmented or incomplete texts. The very act of survival introduces a bias, favoring traditions that for various reasons, left behind a more extensive body of texts. Additionally, our access to this evidence is shaped by many factors. The discovery, preservation, and interpretation of ancient texts are all influenced by modern biases and assumptions. This uneven distribution of evidence, coupled with the limitations of interpreting fragmentary texts, can significantly limit our ability to make comprehensive comparisons. Researchers must always acknowledge these limitations and avoid drawing overly confident conclusions based on incomplete or potentially biased evidence.

It's also essential to address the potential for anachronistic interpretations. Projecting modern concepts and frameworks onto ancient religious beliefs and practices can lead to gross misinterpretations. We must avoid reading our own values, beliefs, and assumptions into ancient texts, instead striving for an understanding grounded in the historical context. For example, interpreting ancient sacrificial rituals through the lens of modern ethical sensibilities can distort their meaning and significance. The same holds true for interpretations of ancient myths and legends. Our contemporary understandings of morality, justice, and social behavior often differ significantly from those of ancient societies, and imposing these modern frameworks can skew our understanding.

In conclusion, while the comparative study of ancient religions offers valuable insights into the human search for meaning and purpose, it is a complex and challenging endeavor. Researchers must navigate a variety of potential pitfalls, including biases, translational difficulties, the limitations of available evidence, and the danger of anachronistic interpretations. By acknowledging and addressing these limitations with humility and critical awareness, researchers can conduct rigorous comparative studies that provide accurate and insightful accounts of the rich diversity and surprising commonalities of ancient religious traditions. The strength of comparative religious studies lies in its ability to uncover significant similarities and striking parallels, but only through rigorous methodology and careful contextualization can these insights genuinely illuminate the complex tapestry of human religious expression. Only through critical self-reflection and a dedication to nuance can we hope to avoid misrepresenting the richness and complexity of these ancient belief systems. The goal is not to force a uniform pattern onto diverse traditions but rather to appreciate the subtle yet profound ways in which humanity has historically grappled with the enduring questions of existence.

Ancient Texts as Sources of Spiritual and Ethical Wisdom

The enduring power of ancient religious texts lies not merely in their historical significance, but in their capacity to offer profound spiritual and ethical wisdom that resonates even today. These texts, born from diverse cultures and spanning millennia, often grapple with fundamental human concerns—the meaning of life, the nature of good and evil, the relationship between humanity and the divine, and the quest for a fulfilling existence. While the specific narratives and rituals may differ drastically, the underlying themes frequently converge, revealing a surprising universality in human spiritual and ethical aspirations.

Consider, for example, the Epic of Gilgamesh, one of the earliest known works of literature. This Mesopotamian epic, predating many other religious texts, explores themes of mortality, friendship, and the search for immortality. Gilgamesh's journey, marked by both triumph and tragedy, reflects a fundamental human desire to transcend the limitations of our earthly existence and grapple with the inevitability of death. While the specifics of Gilgamesh's quest differ from, say, the Buddhist concept of Nirvana or the Christian promise of eternal life, the underlying yearning for something beyond the ephemeral nature of human life is strikingly similar. The text, therefore, provides a window into the timeless human struggle with mortality, a struggle that continues to resonate with readers centuries later. Furthermore, the story’s emphasis on loyalty, friendship, and the consequences of unchecked ambition offer enduring ethical guidance, reflecting the universality of these values across different cultures and times.

Similarly, the Egyptian Book of the Dead, a collection of funerary texts, offers insights into ancient Egyptian beliefs about the afterlife and the ethical principles necessary for a successful passage into the next world. This collection of spells and prayers, intended to guide the deceased through the underworld, reveals a complex cosmology and a sophisticated understanding of ethical conduct. The emphasis on maat, the concept of truth, justice, and cosmic order, highlights the importance of living a morally upright life, even beyond the boundaries of physical existence. While the specifics of the Egyptian afterlife differ from the Christian heaven or the Buddhist reincarnation, the underlying concept of accountability for one's actions and the pursuit of a virtuous life remains a common thread in many religious traditions. The emphasis on confession and accounting for one's actions throughout the Book of the Dead demonstrates an awareness of moral responsibility that is reflected in confessionals and similar practices in many other religious contexts. The detailed instructions and prayers reveal a sophisticated understanding of ethical and spiritual development, showcasing the depth of ancient religious thought.

Moving further east, we find in the Buddhist scriptures, particularly the Dhammapada, a rich tapestry of ethical and spiritual teachings. The Dhammapada, meaning "path of virtue," offers a collection of verses on ethical conduct, mindfulness, and the path to enlightenment. The emphasis on non-violence (ahimsa), compassion (karuna), and mindfulness (sati) provides practical guidance for living a morally upright and spiritually fulfilling life. While the Buddhist path to enlightenment differs significantly from the Abrahamic concept of salvation, the emphasis on ethical conduct and self-cultivation provides a remarkable parallel. The principles of compassion and non-violence found within the Dhammapada echo similar moral imperatives found in other religious and philosophical traditions around the world, emphasizing the commonality of human ethical sensibilities across different cultural backgrounds.

The Abrahamic traditions—Judaism, Christianity, and Islam—also offer a wealth of ethical and spiritual wisdom. The Ten Commandments, a cornerstone of Jewish and Christian ethics, provide a concise yet powerful set of moral principles concerning the relationship between humanity and God and between individuals. These commandments, focusing on issues such as murder, theft, and lying, lay the foundation for a just and equitable society. The emphasis on the importance of respecting parents, adhering to the Sabbath, and not bearing false witness are reflected in similar moral precepts found in other cultures, demonstrating a common understanding of fundamental moral principles across different societies. The Quran, the central religious text of Islam, similarly emphasizes ethical conduct, justice, and compassion. The emphasis on social responsibility, charity (zakat), and the importance of upholding justice are key tenets of Islamic faith, further illustrating the convergence of moral principles across different religious traditions.

The transmission and evolution of these ancient texts are crucial to understanding their enduring relevance. These texts were not static entities but rather evolved over time, reflecting the changing social, political, and cultural contexts in which they existed. Oral traditions, scribal practices, and the process of interpretation all played crucial roles in shaping these texts. The variations and interpretations that arose across different communities and historical periods highlight the dynamic nature of religious belief and practice. This evolution, however, does not diminish the value of these texts. Rather, it enriches our understanding of how religious beliefs have adapted and evolved over time while still retaining core ethical and spiritual principles. Studying the transmission and evolution allows us to trace the development of ethical thought, providing a richer appreciation for the context within which these principles originated and how they have influenced subsequent religious and cultural expressions.

Furthermore, the study of apocryphal and less-known texts from different religious traditions reveals even more remarkable parallels. These texts, often excluded from canonical collections, offer unique perspectives on religious beliefs and practices, revealing alternative interpretations and traditions that may have been marginalized or forgotten. Comparing these less-known texts with the more canonical ones provides a more comprehensive understanding of the diversity and complexity of ancient religious systems. The comparison not only illuminates the variations and contradictions within a given tradition but also highlights unexpected similarities across different cultural and religious contexts. By including these less prominent texts in comparative analysis, researchers can obtain a more holistic and nuanced understanding of ancient religious thought and practice.

The comparison of these ancient texts, therefore, does not aim to homogenize or diminish the rich diversity of religious traditions. Instead, it seeks to identify the shared human concerns and ethical principles that transcend cultural and historical boundaries. These shared concerns, reflected in the remarkable parallels between these seemingly disparate texts, suggest fundamental aspects of the human condition, highlighting the enduring search for meaning, purpose, and moral guidance. The insights gleaned from such a comparative analysis offer not only a profound understanding of the past but also relevant spiritual and ethical guidance for navigating the complexities of the present. These ancient texts provide a rich and enduring resource for anyone seeking to grapple with the fundamental questions of human existence, offering a timeless wellspring of ethical and spiritual wisdom that transcends the boundaries of time and culture. The ongoing relevance of these texts demonstrates the enduring power of human spiritual and ethical aspirations. By understanding the common threads running through these diverse traditions, we can foster a deeper appreciation for the shared humanity that underlies our differences and develop a more compassionate and interconnected world.

The Human Condition Shared Themes Across Cultures and Time Periods

The remarkable convergence of themes across ancient religious texts isn't simply a matter of coincidence; it reflects a shared human experience, a universal grappling with fundamental existential questions that transcends geographical boundaries and historical periods. The search for meaning, a driving force behind much of religious thought, finds expression in diverse forms, yet reveals a striking commonality. The Epic of Gilgamesh, for instance, chronicles a king's desperate quest for immortality, fueled by the fear of death and a desire to leave a lasting legacy. This resonates profoundly with the Buddhist pursuit of Nirvana, a state of liberation from the cycle of suffering and rebirth, albeit achieved through a vastly different path. Similarly, the Abrahamic traditions offer the promise of eternal life, a reward for righteous living, illustrating the widespread human desire for transcendence and enduring existence beyond the confines of mortality. Even the Egyptian Book of the Dead, with its elaborate rituals and spells aimed at securing a successful passage into the afterlife, reflects this fundamental aspiration. The sheer diversity of approaches—physical immortality, spiritual liberation, and eternal reward—highlights the enduring power of this central human yearning.

Furthermore, the pervasive experience of suffering forms a cornerstone of many ancient religious traditions. The pervasiveness of human suffering, from physical pain and loss to existential angst, isn't ignored; rather, it becomes a central focus for reflection and spiritual exploration. In the Buddhist texts, suffering (dukkha) is identified as a fundamental aspect of existence, stemming from attachment and craving. The path to liberation involves cultivating mindfulness, compassion, and detachment to alleviate this suffering. In contrast, the Abrahamic traditions often frame suffering as a test of faith, a trial to be endured with patience and resilience. This suffering, in these traditions, often serves to strengthen faith and deepen one's connection with the divine. The narratives within the Book of Job, for example, directly confront the problem of suffering, illustrating its potential to challenge and even strengthen faith. The various explanations and approaches to suffering reveal a fundamental shared human experience, emphasizing the universality of this struggle.

The conceptualization of good and evil, a crucial element in shaping moral codes and ethical frameworks across cultures, also displays remarkable similarities. While the specific manifestations of good and evil might vary, the underlying dichotomy remains a consistent theme. The Sumerian creation myth, for instance, portrays a battle between order and chaos, representing a fundamental struggle between good and evil forces. This cosmic struggle finds echoes in the Abrahamic traditions, with the conflict between God and Satan reflecting a similar dynamic. The Egyptian concept of Ma'at, encompassing truth, justice, and cosmic order, emphasizes the importance of living a righteous life, mirroring the moral frameworks of numerous other traditions. Even the Dhammapada, with its emphasis on ethical conduct and the cultivation of virtuous qualities, highlights a shared understanding of the importance of moral behavior and its consequences. These examples underscore the universality of moral principles, suggesting that a fundamental sense of right and wrong is an inherent aspect of the human condition.

Finally, the relationship between humanity and the divine or supernatural represents a core element shaping religious beliefs and practices. The nature of the divine, as conceived in ancient texts, varies widely. From the polytheistic pantheons of ancient Greece and Rome to the monotheistic God of the Abrahamic traditions, and the multifaceted concepts within Buddhism and Hinduism, the diverse representations reflect different cultural understandings and cosmological perspectives. However, a common thread persists: the acknowledgment of a power or force beyond human comprehension, a reality that both transcends and interacts with the human realm. In the Epic of Gilgamesh, the gods intervene directly in human affairs, shaping destinies and dispensing rewards and punishments. Similarly, the Egyptian Book of the Dead portrays a complex system of deities and an elaborate underworld journey, highlighting the significant role of the supernatural in shaping the lives and destinies of individuals. The diverse representations of the divine and the varied forms of interaction between humanity and the divine underscore the enduring human inclination to engage with spiritual matters, to seek explanations for the mysteries of existence, and to grapple with the questions of our origins, purposes, and ultimate destinies.

The overarching comparison of these themes—the search for meaning, the experience of suffering, the concepts of good and evil, and the relationship with the divine—reveals a shared human quest for understanding and purpose. These ancient texts, though originating from vastly different cultural contexts and employing unique narrative structures and symbolic language, ultimately reflect a shared human experience, speaking to fundamental anxieties and aspirations that remain relevant even today. The persistent resonance of these themes across millennia underscores the enduring power of these ancient narratives and their capacity to offer insights into the human condition, fostering a deeper understanding of ourselves and our place within the cosmos.

Further exploration into the specific narratives and beliefs of each tradition will illuminate these shared themes in greater detail, revealing the rich tapestry of human spiritual and ethical thought across time and culture. The commonalities found within these diverse traditions provide a foundation for cross-cultural understanding, highlighting the underlying unity of human experience despite the diversity of cultural expressions. The study of these parallels not only sheds light on the past but also offers valuable insights into the ongoing human search for meaning and purpose in the present. By understanding the common threads that unite these diverse traditions, we can move toward a more compassionate and interconnected world, recognizing the shared humanity that underlies our differences.

Overview of the Ancient Traditions Under Consideration

The journey into the heart of ancient religious traditions begins with a necessary overview of the faiths we will explore in detail. Understanding the individual landscapes of belief before comparing them is crucial for a nuanced and accurate analysis. This section, therefore, provides a brief introduction to the Greek, Roman, Egyptian, Buddhist, and Abrahamic traditions, touching upon their historical contexts, core beliefs, and primary sacred texts. This is not an exhaustive study of any single tradition, but rather a preparatory sketch to equip the reader with the necessary background for the comparative analyses that follow.

Let us commence with the ancient Greco-Roman world, a civilization whose influence on Western thought and culture remains profound. Greek religion, characterized by its polytheistic pantheon, featured a rich tapestry of gods and goddesses, each with distinct domains and personalities. Narratives surrounding these deities—found in Homer's *Iliad* and *Odyssey* , Hesiod's *Theogony* , and numerous other myths and legends—reveal complex relationships, moral dilemmas, and heroic struggles. These narratives, often recited and dramatized, played a vital role in shaping Greek society, providing ethical guidelines, explanations for natural phenomena, and a framework for understanding human life and destiny. While lacking a single, unified sacred text comparable to the Bible or the Quran, the accumulated body of Greek mythology and philosophical writings serves as a rich source of insight into their religious beliefs and practices. The Romans, inheriting much of the Greek pantheon and religious practices, adapted and modified them, incorporating indigenous deities and rituals into their own system of belief. Roman religion, while also polytheistic, emphasized the importance of civic duty and piety, with the state playing a significant role in religious life. Texts like Livy's *History of Rome* offer valuable insights into the relationship between religion and the Roman state, revealing the significant role played by religious rituals and festivals in maintaining social order and reinforcing imperial authority.

Turning our attention eastward, ancient Egypt presents a fascinating case study of a civilization deeply intertwined with its religious beliefs. Egyptian religion, characterized by its intricate system of gods and goddesses, elaborate funerary rituals, and a profound belief in the afterlife, left an enduring legacy. The *Book of the Dead* , a collection of spells and prayers intended to guide the deceased through the perilous journey into the underworld, stands as a testament to their belief in immortality and resurrection. Hieroglyphic inscriptions on temple walls and tombs, along with papyri and other artifacts, offer glimpses into the complexities of Egyptian religious thought, revealing a rich tapestry of deities, myths, and rituals. The role of pharaohs as divine intermediaries between the gods and the people, the concept of Ma'at—divine order and justice—and the elaborate beliefs surrounding mummification and the afterlife all contributed to a highly structured and deeply ingrained religious system. The stability and longevity of the Egyptian civilization for millennia are, in no small part, attributable to the pervasive influence of their religious beliefs and practices.

In stark contrast to the polytheistic traditions of Greece, Rome, and Egypt, Buddhism presents a distinct path toward spiritual enlightenment. Originating in India with Siddhartha Gautama (the Buddha), Buddhism focuses on the elimination of suffering through the understanding of impermanence, non-self, and dependent origination. Key texts, such as the

Dhammapada (a collection of verses on ethical conduct and wisdom) and the various sutras (discourses attributed to the Buddha), provide detailed accounts of his teachings, highlighting the path to Nirvana, a state of liberation from the cycle of birth, death, and rebirth. Unlike many other ancient religious systems that emphasize a personal relationship with a god or gods, Buddhism emphasizes self-cultivation and the development of wisdom and compassion through practices like meditation and mindfulness. The emphasis on personal responsibility for one's spiritual growth, the rejection of rigid dogma, and the adaptation of Buddhist principles to diverse cultural contexts contribute to the long and varied history of this influential faith. The spread of Buddhism from India across Asia, its adaptation to different cultures, and its evolution into diverse schools of thought underscore its enduring appeal and flexibility.

Finally, we turn to the Abrahamic traditions—Judaism, Christianity, and Islam—which, despite their historical and theological differences, share a common lineage and a set of foundational beliefs. Judaism, the oldest of these three faiths, emphasizes the covenant between God and the Jewish people, as revealed in the Torah (the first five books of the Hebrew Bible). The Torah contains foundational narratives of creation, the patriarchs, and the exodus from Egypt, laying the groundwork for Jewish law, ethics, and religious practice. The Prophets, chronicled in the subsequent books of the Hebrew Bible, offer further guidance and warnings, emphasizing social justice and God's unwavering commitment to his chosen people. Christianity, originating within Judaism, centers on the figure of Jesus Christ, whom Christians believe to be the Son of God, sent to redeem humanity through his death and resurrection. The New Testament, including the Gospels and the Pauline epistles, provides the foundational texts of Christianity, detailing the life, teachings, and ministry of Jesus, as well as the early development of the Christian church. Islam, the youngest of the Abrahamic faiths, emphasizes the absolute oneness of God (Allah) and the prophethood of Muhammad, who is believed to be the final prophet in a line extending back to Abraham. The Quran, considered the literal word of God, serves as the central text of Islam, providing guidance on all aspects of life, from worship and ethics to social and political matters. The Hadith, collections of sayings and traditions attributed to Muhammad, provide further elucidation and interpretation of the Quran's teachings.

This overview provides a starting point for our exploration into the fascinating similarities and differences among these ancient religious traditions. Each of these traditions—Greek, Roman, Egyptian, Buddhist, and Abrahamic—offers a unique window into human spirituality, ethical systems, and the perennial search for meaning and purpose. The following chapters will delve deeper into the specifics of these traditions, examining their sacred texts, theological concepts, and historical development, providing a rich foundation for the comparative analysis that follows. The careful consideration of each tradition's unique characteristics will not only enhance our understanding of their individual legacies but also illuminate the surprising parallels that ultimately bind them together. The common threads that emerge, despite their diverse contexts and beliefs, offer compelling insights into the enduring aspects of the human condition and the timeless search for universal truths. The subsequent chapters will uncover these profound connections, revealing the remarkable convergence of human aspirations across vastly different cultures and times.

Comparing Creation Myths from Mesopotamia and Egypt

Delving into the origins of the cosmos, we now turn our attention to two ancient civilizations whose creation myths offer compelling insights into their respective worldviews: Mesopotamia and Egypt. While geographically distinct and possessing unique cultural identities, their creation narratives reveal surprising parallels alongside significant differences, shedding light on the human impulse to explain the universe's origins and humanity's place within it.

Mesopotamia, the land between the rivers Tigris and Euphrates, cradled a vibrant array of cultures and civilizations, each contributing to a rich tapestry of mythological narratives. Among the most well-known Mesopotamian creation myths is the *Enuma Elish* , a Babylonian epic poem dating back to the late second millennium BCE. This epic unfolds a dramatic cosmic battle, a primordial chaos preceding the ordered universe we inhabit. The *Enuma Elish* portrays a watery abyss teeming with monstrous deities, the Apsu (freshwater) and Tiamat (saltwater), embodying the formless void from which all things would emerge. Their union produces a younger generation of gods, whose boisterous activities disturb the peace of their parents. Apsu, seeking to destroy his unruly offspring, plots with Tiamat, leading to a rebellion spearheaded by the god Marduk.

Marduk, a relatively young and ambitious deity, is chosen by the other gods to confront Tiamat. The epic depicts a thrilling battle, full of vivid imagery and dramatic tension, where Marduk ultimately triumphs over the primordial goddess. He then proceeds to dissect Tiamat's body, fashioning the heavens and the earth from her remains. This act of violent creation underscores the Mesopotamian worldview, where order is achieved through the conquest of chaos. The heavens are created from Tiamat's upper body, the earth from her lower, and humanity is fashioned from the blood of Kingu, Tiamat's consort. This creation narrative is far from benevolent; it's a tale of power struggles, violent conquest, and the establishment of order through force. The cosmos is not a gentle creation but a battleground, reflecting a world where survival depended on strength and strategic alliances.

The *Enuma Elish* also provides a cosmogony, a model of the universe's structure. The cosmos is viewed as a layered structure, with the earth at the center, surrounded by the heavens, and the underworld below. This hierarchical arrangement mirrors the social structure of Mesopotamian society, where power was concentrated at the top, reflecting a divinely ordained order. The gods themselves are hierarchical, with Marduk ascending to the supreme position after his victory over Tiamat. The creation of humanity, derived from the blood of a defeated enemy, implies a subservient role for humankind, created to serve the gods and maintain the cosmic order. This understanding of humanity’s purpose is deeply ingrained in the narrative structure, revealing a worldview that emphasizes order, hierarchy, and the ever-present threat of chaos. The epic also highlights the cyclical nature of time; the gods themselves are subject to change and power struggles, mirroring the dynamism of the Mesopotamian world.

In stark contrast to the violent chaos of the *Enuma Elish* , Egyptian creation myths often present a more peaceful and orderly emergence of the cosmos. The Ogdoad myth, for instance, offers a contrasting perspective. This creation narrative, originating from Hermopolis, depicts the creation emerging from a primordial watery abyss, but unlike the Babylonian narrative, this abyss is not chaotic and violent, but a source of potential and generative force. The Ogdoad consists of eight deities, four pairs of complementary deities representing the primordial forces: Nun (primordial water), Naunet (primordial darkness), Huh (infinity), and Hauhet (eternity). These four pairs represent the duality inherent in creation, the interplay of contrasting forces leading to the generation of life. These primordial forces were not involved in conflict but acted in harmony to give birth to the cosmos.

Unlike the *Enuma Elish* 's dramatic battle scene, the Ogdoad myth depicts a more gradual and peaceful emergence of order from primordial chaos. From the union of these deities, Atum, the creator god, emerges, often depicted as a self-created being emerging from the primordial waters. He then creates the world through acts of masturbation or spitting – symbolic of generative power – bringing forth Shu (air) and Tefnut (moisture). This act, while unusual by modern standards, underscores the generative principle of creation. Shu and Tefnut, in turn, give birth to Geb (earth) and Nut (sky), who, according to some versions, are the parents of the next generation of gods, the Ennead.

The Ogdoad myth presents a fundamentally different cosmogony than the *Enuma Elish* . While the Mesopotamian narrative emphasizes a hierarchical order established through conquest, the Egyptian myth emphasizes a more balanced and harmonious creation. The creation process itself is not violent but a result of inherent generative forces, symbolizing the natural processes of the world. The cyclical nature of time is also evident, with different generations of gods influencing and shaping the world. Humanity's role in this cosmology is not explicitly defined in the Ogdoad myth in the same way as in the *Enuma Elish* , but the emphasis on

Ma'at, the concept of divine order and justice, suggests a harmonious coexistence between humanity and the divine.

Comparing these two creation narratives highlights the diverse ways in which ancient cultures sought to understand the origins of the universe and humanity's place within it. The *Enuma Elish* reflects a worldview shaped by conflict, where order emerges from chaos through force and conquest. The Ogdoad myth, on the other hand, presents a more harmonious creation, where order arises from the interaction of complementary forces. These differences reflect not only the distinct cultural contexts of Mesopotamia and Egypt but also the varied ways in which humanity has grappled with the fundamental questions of existence, revealing the enduring power of mythology to reflect and shape our understanding of the world. The contrasting emphasis on violence versus harmony highlights the diverse ways in which ancient cultures constructed their narratives, reflecting their own social structures and values. The study of these myths offers invaluable insights into the minds of these ancient civilizations, enriching our comprehension of the human condition and our timeless search for understanding of our origins. Further comparative analysis with other creation myths will continue to illuminate this fascinating interplay of beliefs and narratives across diverse cultures.

Analyzing Creation Narratives in the Abrahamic Traditions

The exploration of creation myths continues with a focused examination of the Abrahamic traditions – Judaism, Christianity, and Islam. These faiths, while sharing a common ancestor in their belief in a single, omnipotent God, present nuanced variations in their respective creation narratives. Understanding these nuances allows for a deeper appreciation of the theological underpinnings of each religion and the development of their respective cosmologies. The Book of Genesis, the foundational text of the Hebrew Bible and a cornerstone of both Judaism and Christianity, offers perhaps the most widely recognized account.

Genesis presents a remarkably concise and elegant creation narrative, structured in six days of divine activity culminating in the creation of humanity. Day one witnesses the creation of light and the separation of light from darkness, establishing a fundamental cosmic order. Day two sees the creation of the firmament, separating the waters above from the waters below, a separation that continues to resonate in symbolic interpretations. Day three marks the creation of dry land, vegetation, and the beginnings of biological life. Day four introduces celestial bodies – the sun, moon, and stars – to regulate time and mark the seasons. Day five brings forth aquatic and avian life, further diversifying the created world. Finally, on day six, God creates land animals and culminates His work with the creation of humanity, male and female, in His own image. This act of creation is presented as a culmination, a pinnacle of God's creative power, bestowing upon humanity a unique status and responsibility within the created order. The seventh day is a day of rest, a divine act of cessation emphasizing the completeness and perfection of creation.

The language used in Genesis is remarkably evocative. God's actions are described with simple yet powerful verbs, conveying a sense of divine power and intentionality. Phrases like "God said, 'Let there be light,' and there was light" emphasize the immediate and absolute nature of divine creation, emphasizing the divine power of speech and fiat. The repeated phrase "And God saw that it was good" underscores the divine approval of each stage of creation, highlighting the inherent goodness and perfection of God's design. This inherent goodness becomes a crucial element in understanding the theological perspective of the Abrahamic faiths. The creation of humanity in God's image carries profound implications, imbuing humanity with unique dignity and responsibilities, establishing a special relationship between creator and creation. This relationship, however, is also one of accountability, implying a moral obligation to steward the created world.

The Quran, the central religious text of Islam, presents a different, yet complementary, narrative of creation. While it echoes certain aspects of the Genesis account, it emphasizes different theological themes and offers a unique perspective on the role of God and humanity in the cosmos. The Quranic account, spread across various verses, does not adhere to the strict six-day framework of Genesis. It emphasizes the swiftness and power of God's creation, often using evocative imagery to describe the creation of the heavens and the earth, often from nothingness or a primordial void. The Quran highlights God's omnipotence and transcendence, emphasizing the ease with which He created the universe and all its inhabitants. Like Genesis, the Quran emphasizes the creation of humanity, often describing it as the culmination of God's creative act, although the creation of

Adam and Eve are not explicitly detailed in the same manner. The emphasis is placed more on God's power and wisdom in the creation of humanity.

A significant difference lies in the Quran's focus on the unity and absolute power of God. While Genesis emphasizes the distinct acts of creation on each day, the Quranic narrative often emphasizes the seamless and swift nature of God's creative work. The emphasis is less on the chronological details and more on the majesty and power of God, illustrating His absolute sovereignty over creation. This focus on divine oneness directly counters the potential for polytheism, a central concern in Islamic theology. The concept of God's creative power is repeatedly emphasized through metaphors and similes, utilizing imagery drawn from the natural world to illustrate the divine capacity.

Comparing the divine language used in Genesis and the Quran reveals further distinctions. While Genesis employs a more narrative and descriptive style, the Quran often utilizes a more lyrical and poetic approach. The Quranic verses often utilize evocative imagery and powerful metaphors to convey the grandeur and magnificence of God's creative act. The repetition of divine names and attributes underscores the absolute power and sovereignty of God. The language of the Quran aims to inspire awe and reverence for God's creative power, emphasizing the spiritual and emotional connection between humanity and God.

The differing emphasis in both accounts, though seemingly disparate, can be interpreted as complimentary. Genesis offers a detailed, chronological account emphasizing the order and process of creation, whereas the Quran emphasizes the absolute power and oneness of God, prioritizing the divine act of creation over its precise mechanics. Both texts ultimately affirm the belief in a single, omnipotent God who created the universe and humanity. The subtle differences reflect the unique cultural and historical contexts in which they were written, further highlighting the diversity of expression within a shared theological foundation.

Beyond Genesis and the Quran, other Abrahamic texts, including various apocryphal and pseudepigraphical writings, offer alternative or supplementary accounts of creation. These texts, while not considered canonical in the same way as Genesis or the Quran, provide valuable insights into the development and evolution of creation narratives within the Abrahamic traditions. These texts often incorporate mythological or folkloric elements, sometimes blending these with theological concepts, offering diverse perspectives on the creation of the cosmos and humanity's place within it. Studying these diverse accounts expands our understanding of the fluidity and dynamic evolution of religious thought throughout history.

Analysis of these varied creation narratives within the Abrahamic traditions reveals a complex interplay of theological perspectives and literary styles. While the fundamental belief in a single God who created the universe remains constant, the specific details and emphases vary significantly. Understanding these nuances enriches our comprehension of the individual religious traditions, clarifying the development of their respective cosmologies and worldviews. The comparison reveals not only the shared belief in divine creation but also the varied ways in which this belief has been expressed and interpreted throughout history, reflecting the diversity within a shared theological foundation. Further exploration of these narratives, considering their historical and cultural contexts, is crucial to gain a nuanced appreciation of the depth and complexity of the Abrahamic faiths. The continued comparison with other religious traditions can highlight further parallels and divergences in understanding the origins of the universe and the role of humanity.

The Buddhist Concept of Dependent Origination

The exploration of creation myths and cosmologies thus far has focused on linear narratives, often featuring a singular creator deity and a sequential unfolding of the universe. However, Buddhism, with its rich philosophical and metaphysical framework, offers a radically different perspective, one that eschews the concept of a creator god altogether and replaces it with the concept of dependent origination (pratītyasamutpāda). This concept, central to Buddhist cosmology, provides a powerful alternative to the theistic creation narratives examined previously. Instead of a beginning point, dependent origination posits a dynamic, interconnected web of existence, where everything arises in dependence upon something else. There is no singular, ultimate cause or creator, but rather a continuous cycle of arising and ceasing, of cause and effect.

Understanding dependent origination requires a shift away from the linear, causal model prevalent in many creation myths. These myths often depict a creator god who brings the universe into being *ex nihilo* – from nothing – or from a pre-existing chaotic state. Time is understood as linear, progressing from a beginning to an end. Dependent origination, in contrast, presents a cyclical and relational view of existence. It describes how phenomena arise not from a single source but from a complex interplay of factors, a web of interconnectedness where every element is both cause and effect.

The concept is often illustrated through the metaphor of a chain of links, each link representing a condition or factor contributing to the arising of the next. This chain is not static; it is constantly moving, with links continually appearing and disappearing. The traditional formulation of dependent origination, as found in various Buddhist sutras, usually outlines twelve interconnected factors: ignorance, volitional formations, consciousness, name and form, the six sense bases, contact, feeling, craving, clinging, becoming, birth, and old age and death. This cyclical process, known as *samsara* , is seen as the root of suffering, characterized by impermanence (anicca), suffering (dukkha), and non-self (anatta).

Ignorance, the first link, refers to a lack of understanding of the true nature of reality – the impermanence and interconnectedness of all things. This ignorance leads to volitional formations, which are mental and emotional patterns shaping our perceptions and actions. These formations give rise to consciousness, the awareness of the world around us. Consciousness, combined with various mental and physical factors, manifests as "name and form," referring to the individual's physical and mental characteristics. This combination interacts with the six sense bases – the five senses plus the mind – leading to contact, the interaction between sense organs and objects. Contact produces feelings, which can be pleasurable, painful, or neutral. These feelings lead to craving, the desire for pleasurable experiences and the avoidance of painful ones. Craving leads to clinging, the attachment to things and experiences. Clinging generates "becoming," the continuous cycle of rebirth, driven by the desire to maintain pleasurable experiences and avoid suffering. Becoming results in birth, the emergence of a new individual, and this eventually leads to old age and death. The cycle then repeats, driven by the ongoing ignorance of the true nature of reality.

The absence of a creator god in the Buddhist cosmology distinguishes it sharply from the theistic creation myths previously discussed. While the Abrahamic traditions posit a

God who intentionally creates the universe and humanity, Buddhism emphasizes the inherent interconnectedness and interdependence of all things. There is no singular agent initiating the process; rather, the whole of existence is a dynamic interplay of causes and effects, none of which is ultimately the singular origin.

Furthermore, the Buddhist concept of impermanence challenges the notion of a fixed and eternal creation, commonly found in many creation myths. The creation narratives examined earlier often depict a creation that, while potentially subject to decay or destruction, maintains a fundamental underlying order and essence. In contrast, Buddhism emphasizes the impermanent nature of all phenomena, stating that everything is in a constant state of flux and change. Nothing remains the same; everything is transient and subject to decay. Even the universe itself is not considered permanent but rather a temporary manifestation of dependent origination.

This emphasis on impermanence also profoundly impacts the Buddhist understanding of self. The concept of "anatta," or non-self, directly contradicts the notion of an enduring, unchanging soul or essence that many creation myths imply. The idea of a creator often goes hand-in-hand with the concept of a created individual possessing a fixed, eternal identity. But Buddhist philosophy emphasizes that there is no permanent, unchanging self; rather, the individual is a constantly changing aggregation of physical and mental processes, a temporary confluence of factors arising from dependent origination.

This concept significantly impacts ethics and morality in Buddhism. Since there is no inherent self, actions are seen not as belonging to a permanent entity, but as products of various conditions and causes. Karma, the law of cause and effect, becomes pivotal, as it highlights the consequences of one's actions on oneself and others within this interconnected web of existence. Ethical behavior, therefore, is not merely a matter of obedience to divine command but of understanding the consequences of one's actions within the framework of dependent origination, aiming for actions that minimize suffering and promote harmony.

Another important distinction arises from the Buddhist concept of Nirvana, the ultimate goal of Buddhist practice. Nirvana is not a creation or a place, but rather a state of liberation from the cycle of samsara, achieved by understanding and transcending the mechanisms of dependent origination. It’s a cessation of suffering, achieved through the cessation of craving and clinging, a transcendence of the very process that drives the cycle of birth, death, and rebirth. This differs greatly from the concept of a divinely-ordained paradise or afterlife found in many creation narratives.

The comparison of dependent origination with the linear creation narratives of other traditions highlights the diverse ways in which humanity has attempted to make sense of existence and its origins. While creation myths often provide comforting narratives of a benevolent creator establishing order from chaos, dependent origination offers a more complex, less anthropocentric view, emphasizing the dynamic, interconnected, and impermanent nature of reality. It is not a story of creation in the traditional sense, but rather a framework for understanding the processes of arising and ceasing, offering a profound exploration of causality, suffering, and liberation. This understanding fundamentally reshapes our perception of the universe, of ourselves, and of our place within the larger cosmic order. The stark contrasts between the viewpoints presented by dependent origination and traditional creation myths underscore the profound differences in worldviews and fundamental assumptions about the nature of reality. Further study of these differences allows for a more nuanced understanding of the rich tapestry of human spiritual thought. The lack of a singular creator and the focus on the impermanent nature of all things provides a radically different framework for understanding human existence, offering alternative avenues to comprehend both the universe's origins and humanity's place within it. This comparative analysis provides a rich basis for exploring the diverse ways in which different religious traditions approach the fundamental questions surrounding existence and our place within it.

Greek and Roman Cosmogonies and their Influence

The shift from the cyclical and interconnected cosmology of Buddhism to the more linear and hierarchical systems of the Greeks and Romans reveals a fascinating divergence in approaches to understanding the universe's origins. While Buddhism eschews a creator deity, Greek and Roman cosmogonies are deeply intertwined with a pantheon of gods and goddesses, each with distinct roles in shaping the cosmos and the lives of mortals. These narratives, passed down through generations via myths, poems, and philosophical treatises, offer a rich tapestry of creation accounts, highlighting the influence of cultural and societal structures on religious beliefs.

The most widely known Greek cosmogony centers around the Olympian pantheon, a group of twelve major deities residing on Mount Olympus. Hesiod's *Theogony* , a foundational text in Greek mythology, provides a detailed genealogy of the gods, tracing their lineage back to primordial beings like Gaia (Earth) and Uranus (Sky). From this primal union sprung the Titans, a powerful generation of gods, who in turn were overthrown by their children, the Olympians, led by Zeus, king of the gods. This narrative of rebellion and succession reveals a dynamic, even violent, struggle for cosmic dominance, a far cry from the serene, orderly creation often depicted in other traditions. The creation itself wasn't a singular event but a series of transformative events, each marked by power struggles and the establishment of a new order.

Zeus's role in the Greek cosmos is central to understanding their creation narrative. He wasn't simply a creator *ex nihilo* , but a powerful figure who established order amidst chaos, overthrowing his father and subjugating the Titans. His actions shaped the structure of the universe, establishing the realms of the heavens, the earth, and the underworld. His authority extended over the other gods, mortals, and even the natural forces of the cosmos. This powerful, anthropomorphic deity differed significantly from the more abstract and less interventionist creator gods found in certain other traditions.

Beyond Zeus, other Olympian gods played significant roles in shaping the Greek cosmos. Poseidon, brother of Zeus, controlled the seas, shaping the land through earthquakes and tsunamis. Hades, another brother, ruled the underworld, a realm as much a part of the cosmos as the world of the living. Hestia, goddess of the hearth, represented the domestic sphere and the stability of the home, reflecting the importance of family and community within Greek society. Hera, Zeus's wife, embodied marriage, women, and family, while Aphrodite, goddess of love and beauty, played a pivotal role in shaping human relationships. Each deity possessed a specific domain of influence, reflecting the interconnectedness of different aspects of life within the Greek worldview. The Olympian pantheon wasn't simply a collection of independent entities, but a hierarchical system with interconnected domains of influence, reflecting a complex and stratified societal structure.

Roman mythology, while influenced significantly by Greek narratives, also features its own distinct pantheon and cosmogonies. While many Roman gods were directly equated with their Greek counterparts (e.g., Jupiter with Zeus, Neptune with Poseidon, Pluto with Hades), their narratives and functions were often subtly reinterpreted to reflect Roman values and cultural priorities. Roman myths tend to emphasize order, stability, and the rule of law, reflecting the highly structured nature of Roman society. The emphasis on practical matters and civic virtue is quite different from the more dramatic and sometimes chaotic narratives of Greek mythology.

The Roman creation myth often begins with the primordial gods, Caelus (Sky) and Terra (Earth), and their offspring. These gods, comparable to the Greek Titans, eventually gave way to a new generation, led by Jupiter, the Roman equivalent of Zeus. However, the Roman narratives generally focus less on violent conflict and more on the establishment of order and the creation of the Roman state itself. The emphasis shifts from individual gods' heroic deeds to the establishment and maintenance of cosmic order, reflecting Roman preoccupation with civic duty and the stability of the empire. This reflected the Roman political structure where power was less about individual heroism and more about maintaining a well-ordered state.

Comparing the Greek and Roman cosmogonies with other creation myths reveals both similarities and differences. The emphasis on powerful anthropomorphic deities is a recurring theme, contrasting with the more abstract conceptions of divinity found in certain Eastern traditions. However, the specific roles and relationships of these deities, as well as the overall structure of the cosmos, reflect the unique cultural values and societal structures of the Greek and Roman civilizations. The hierarchical structure of the pantheons mirrors the social hierarchies of their respective societies. The focus on the establishment of order after a period of chaos, a common element in many creation myths, appears in Greek and Roman narratives, but with distinct emphases. In the Greek narrative, it's a more chaotic and violent process, a fight for dominance, whereas in the Roman narrative, it's a more orderly and structured transition.

The influence of Greek and Roman cosmogonies on later Western thought is undeniable. The Olympian pantheon and its stories permeated literature, art, and philosophy for centuries. The concepts of fate, destiny, and divine intervention, prominent in these myths, deeply affected Western philosophical and theological thought. The legacy of these gods and their narratives can be seen in countless works of art, literature, and even modern-day culture. Their names and stories resonate through Western culture, shaping our language, artistic expressions, and collective imagination. This persistent influence underscores the enduring power of these narratives to shape human understanding of the world and our place within it.

Moreover, the classical cosmogonies provide valuable insights into the human condition. The struggles of the gods, their flaws, and their triumphs mirror the human experience, illustrating the eternal themes of power, ambition, love, loss, and mortality. The complexities of the relationships among the deities reflect the complexities of human relationships. The classical myths serve as a powerful exploration of the human psyche and the enduring quest for meaning and purpose.

The examination of Greek and Roman cosmogonies, therefore, offers a valuable perspective on the evolution of religious thought. By comparing and contrasting their creation narratives with those of other cultures, we gain a deeper appreciation for the diversity of human belief systems and the ways in which they reflect the unique experiences and values of their respective societies. The differences and similarities highlight the enduring human need to understand the origins of the universe and our place within the cosmic order, showcasing the diverse pathways humanity has taken in its quest for meaning and understanding. The enduring legacy of these narratives serves as a powerful testament to their ability to resonate across cultures and time periods.

Synthesizing Creation Narratives Common Themes and Variations

The diverse tapestry of creation myths woven throughout human history, from the ancient civilizations of Mesopotamia to the philosophical traditions of the East, reveals a remarkable underlying unity despite their surface differences. While the specific details vary dramatically – from the chaotic churning of primordial waters in Babylonian accounts to the divine fiat of the Abrahamic traditions – a closer examination reveals recurring themes that speak to fundamental aspects of the human condition and our enduring quest to understand our place in the cosmos.

One of the most pervasive themes is the transition from chaos to order. In the Enuma Elish, the Babylonian creation epic, the universe begins as a watery abyss, a formless void populated by warring deities. From this primordial chaos, Marduk, the chief god, emerges victorious, imposing order and structure on the cosmos. This motif is echoed in the Greek creation narrative, where the Olympian gods overthrow the Titans, establishing a new hierarchical order. Similarly, the Egyptian creation myth features a gradual emergence of order from the primordial waters of Nun, culminating in the creation of the world and the establishment of Ma'at, the principle of cosmic harmony. Even in seemingly dissimilar traditions like the indigenous creation stories of various cultures worldwide, one finds this constant movement from a state of formlessness and disorder towards a structured and organized reality. This common thread suggests a fundamental human desire to impose order on the perceived chaos of existence, a deep-seated need to find structure and meaning in a world that can often feel unpredictable and overwhelming.

Another recurring theme is the role of a creator deity or force. While the nature of this deity varies significantly, the concept of a divine being or power responsible for initiating creation is widespread. The Abrahamic traditions emphasize a singular, all-powerful God who creates the universe *ex nihilo* , from nothing. In contrast, many polytheistic traditions depict a pantheon of gods and goddesses who collectively shape the cosmos, each with their own domain of influence. Even in traditions that eschew a personal creator god, such as Buddhism, a cosmic principle or process is often invoked to explain the origins of the universe. This shared emphasis on a creator, whether singular or plural, reflects a deeply ingrained human tendency to attribute ultimate causality to a transcendent source, a need to explain the origin of existence beyond the realm of the mundane. The diversity of forms this creator takes mirrors the diverse cultural contexts and philosophical perspectives through which humanity has grappled with these fundamental questions.

The concept of primordial matter also emerges as a recurring motif. The concept of a pre-existing substance, from which the universe is formed, appears in diverse mythologies. In some traditions, this takes the form of a cosmic egg or a world tree. In others, it may be represented as chaotic waters, a formless void, or a primordial mountain. These symbols signify an undefined, pre-structured state that precedes the organized universe we inhabit. The act of creation, then, is viewed as the shaping or organizing of this primordial matter, bringing forth order and structure from an initial state of potentiality. The various symbolic representations of this primordial material reflect the varying cultural interpretations of the pre-existent state of reality and highlight the significance of the transformation from formlessness to form.

Furthermore, the creation narratives often contain elements of sacrifice and struggle. In many myths, the creation of the world is achieved through acts of divine sacrifice or through violent conflicts between powerful beings. The Babylonian Enuma Elish depicts Marduk slaying Tiamat, the primordial sea monster, and using her body to create the world. Similarly, the Greek creation myth features a series of conflicts and power struggles among the gods. Even in more peaceful narratives, the act of creation itself often involves a form of sacrifice, a relinquishing of something precious to bring about a new order. This underscores the idea that creation is not a passive process but one that requires effort, sacrifice, and possibly even conflict to achieve. The repeated motif of sacrifice highlights the fundamental understanding that the formation of order, whether cosmic or societal, might demand a relinquishing of aspects of the previous state.

The creation narratives also reflect the cultural values and societal structures of the societies that produced them. The hierarchical nature of many creation myths, with powerful creator deities at the apex, mirrors the social hierarchies of the societies that created them. For example, the rigidly structured nature of ancient Egyptian society is mirrored in their creation narratives, where the gods are arranged in a clear hierarchy. In contrast, the more egalitarian nature of some indigenous cultures is reflected in their creation myths, which often feature a collaborative process of creation rather than a single, dominant creator figure. This connection between creation myths and societal structures demonstrates how religious beliefs are often intertwined with cultural values and social organization, highlighting the profound influence of cultural context on religious expression. The creation myth is not simply a narrative about the origin of the universe; it is also a reflection of the society that tells it.

Finally, the enduring power of creation myths lies in their ability to provide answers to fundamental questions about existence. These narratives offer explanations for the origin of the universe, humankind, and the world around us. They provide a framework for understanding our place within the cosmos, the purpose of life, and the nature of morality. The persistence of these myths across diverse cultures and throughout history suggests their fundamental importance in shaping human understanding, providing comfort, hope, and a sense of meaning in the face of existential uncertainty. The continued relevance of creation narratives highlights the enduring human need to make sense of the world and our place within it. In their various forms, these myths represent attempts to grapple with fundamental questions that have resonated across millennia, connecting humanity across different times and places. The variations highlight the adaptability of these stories, reflecting the changing cultural values, societal structures, and philosophical viewpoints of the different societies that transmit them.

In conclusion, while creation narratives differ dramatically in their specific details, a careful comparative analysis reveals remarkable commonalities. The recurring themes of chaos to order, creator deities, primordial matter, sacrifice and struggle, and the reflection of cultural values suggest fundamental aspects of the human experience and our enduring quest to understand our origins and our place within the universe. The enduring power of these narratives speaks to the persistent human need to find meaning, purpose, and understanding in the face of the vast unknown. The diversity of these myths should be appreciated not just as different narratives but as diverse expressions of the same fundamental human drive to comprehend our place in existence.

The Epic of Gilgamesh and the Great Flood

The Epic of Gilgamesh, a cornerstone of Mesopotamian literature, offers a compelling version of the deluge myth, adding layers of complexity and human drama to the archetypal flood narrative. Unlike simpler accounts that merely recount the divine decision to flood the earth and the survival of a chosen few, Gilgamesh's flood narrative is embedded within a larger epic that explores themes of mortality, friendship, and the search for meaning in a seemingly chaotic world. This integration enriches the flood story, transforming it from a simple recounting of divine wrath into a profound reflection on the human condition.

The narrative focuses on Utnapishtim, a figure remarkably similar to Noah in the Judeo-Christian tradition. However, Utnapishtim’s story is not simply one of passive obedience to a divine command. Instead, he is portrayed as a shrewd and resourceful individual who, warned of the impending catastrophe by the god Ea, actively takes steps to ensure his survival and the preservation of life. This proactive role sets him apart from other figures in flood myths who often appear as more passive recipients of divine grace. The details of Utnapishtim’s actions are crucial to understanding the narrative’s significance. He receives specific instructions from Ea, not only regarding the construction of the ark but also concerning the gathering of animals and provisions. This precision highlights the meticulous nature of the preparation, emphasizing the gravity of the impending event and the thoroughness required for survival.

The description of the ark itself is striking. It's not just a vessel; it's a meticulously constructed structure of precise dimensions, designed to withstand the immense power of the flood. The meticulous nature of its construction reflects the seriousness of the task and the detailed planning required to survive the divine wrath. This meticulousness, detailed in the epic, contrasts with some other flood accounts which offer less detail regarding the ark's construction. This contrast underscores the literary sophistication of the Gilgamesh epic and its focus on the practical aspects of survival in the face of catastrophe.

The flood itself is depicted with raw power and terrifying imagery. The text describes the unrelenting rain, the rising waters engulfing the land, and the utter devastation that follows. The vividness of the descriptions paints a picture of a world consumed by chaos, emphasizing the destructive power of the divine intervention. This depiction is not merely a recounting of events; it is a visceral representation of the forces of nature unleashed, reflecting a profound respect, or perhaps even fear, of the divine power capable of such destruction. This stark contrast between the meticulous planning and the overwhelming power of nature serves to highlight the vulnerability of humanity even when facing the odds with careful preparation.

Furthermore, the narrative doesn't shy away from portraying the emotional toll of the flood. Utnapishtim, despite his preparedness, experiences the overwhelming terror of witnessing the destruction of his world. This humanization of Utnapishtim makes the narrative more relatable and less of a purely theological tale. The epic does not simply celebrate the survival of the righteous; it also portrays the existential anxiety and the emotional burden of witnessing such widespread devastation. The inclusion of these human elements elevates the story beyond a mere account of divine judgment and into a profound exploration of human resilience in the face of unimaginable hardship.

Upon surviving the flood, Utnapishtim’s story takes a significant turn. He and his family emerge from the ark into a world transformed, a world cleansed but also profoundly altered. The narrative doesn't end with the simple act of survival. It continues to explore Utnapishtim's subsequent experiences and his encounter with Gilgamesh. This post-flood narrative further complicates the story, suggesting the ongoing consequences of divine action and the enduring impact of trauma. This further distinguishes the Gilgamesh flood narrative from simpler accounts that end with the survivors repopulating the earth.

Utnapishtim's encounter with Gilgamesh is pivotal. Gilgamesh, seeking immortality, has travelled far and wide in his quest, and Utnapishtim becomes a crucial figure in his journey. Utnapishtim's story serves not merely as a cautionary tale, but also as a key element in Gilgamesh's own personal transformation. By narrating his experience to Gilgamesh, Utnapishtim imparts a valuable lesson about the nature of mortality and the futility of seeking eternal life. This interaction highlights the thematic interconnectedness of the flood narrative with the larger epic, demonstrating how the experience of the deluge shapes Gilgamesh's understanding of life, death, and the meaning of human existence.

The significance of the flood narrative within the Epic of Gilgamesh extends beyond the simple recounting of a divine punishment. It serves as a pivotal point in the epic's larger thematic trajectory. The flood, as a cataclysmic event, is intertwined with the themes of mortality, the limits of human power, and the acceptance of fate. The flood is not just a random event; it is a crucial catalyst that shapes Gilgamesh's journey and leads him towards a deeper understanding of his own mortality and the acceptance of his place in the cosmic order.

The literary and cultural context of the flood narrative within the Epic of Gilgamesh must also be examined. The epic existed within a specific cultural and historical setting, reflecting the anxieties and beliefs of the Mesopotamian people. The flood could be interpreted as reflecting the real-life experiences of floods that ravaged the Mesopotamian civilization, turning a potentially devastating natural event into a powerful symbolic narrative. The act of divine punishment, described within the epic, can also be understood as representing the unpredictable nature of the world and the limitations of human power in the face of powerful forces of nature. The narrative provides a sense of order and meaning to the seemingly unpredictable events of the natural world.

The comparison of the Gilgamesh flood narrative with other ancient flood myths further enriches our understanding of its significance. While sharing common elements with the biblical flood narrative, for example, the Gilgamesh version differs significantly in its narrative structure, its characterization of the survivors, and its integration within a broader epic narrative. These differences highlight the cultural and literary variations in how different societies have interpreted the archetype of the deluge, emphasizing the diverse ways in which this primordial myth has been adapted and reinterpreted across cultures and across time. The Gilgamesh version, with its human-centric focus and its exploration of complex themes, stands out as a particularly sophisticated and nuanced treatment of the archetypal flood narrative.

The lingering impact of the flood narrative on the later traditions is significant. The story of Utnapishtim and the deluge resonated with many subsequent cultures and civilizations, influencing later versions of the flood myth found in other religious and literary traditions. The story's enduring influence emphasizes its powerful and enduring impact on the human imagination. The parallel narratives in various religious and literary traditions across the globe highlight the universality of this motif.

In conclusion, the flood narrative in the Epic of Gilgamesh is far more than a simple retelling of a divine punishment. It's a complex and multifaceted story that deeply explores the human condition, the limits of human power, and the enduring search for meaning in a world marked by both chaos and order. Its literary sophistication, its rich character development, and its thoughtful exploration of existential themes solidify its place as a crucial and enduring contribution to the vast and varied tapestry of human flood narratives. The epic serves as a testament to the enduring human fascination with the power of nature and our capacity to adapt and endure even in the face of unimaginable destruction. The profound integration of the flood story within the larger narrative of Gilgamesh's journey elevates the myth beyond the realm of a mere religious tale; it becomes a profound exploration of human mortality, resilience, and the ongoing search for purpose and meaning in a world characterized by both chaos and order.

The Biblical Flood Narrative and its Interpretations

The Biblical flood narrative, as recounted in the Book of Genesis, stands as a cornerstone of Judeo-Christian theology and a significant contribution to the global tapestry of deluge myths. While sharing striking similarities with the Epic of Gilgamesh's flood story, the Genesis account possesses distinct characteristics that warrant careful consideration. Unlike the more nuanced portrayal of Utnapishtim, Noah is presented as a righteous man, chosen by God for his unwavering piety. God's command to Noah is direct and unambiguous: to build an ark of specific dimensions and to gather pairs of all living creatures, both clean and unclean. This stark contrast in the presentation of the protagonists highlights differing cultural values and interpretations of the divine-human relationship. In the Gilgamesh epic, the protagonist demonstrates proactive engagement with the divine warning, whereas Noah's role is primarily one of passive obedience.

The Genesis narrative lacks the detailed description of ark construction found in Gilgamesh. While the dimensions are specified, the focus is less on the practicalities of building and provisioning the ark and more on the divine mandate and Noah's obedience. This difference reflects varying literary styles and theological priorities. The Gilgamesh epic, rooted in a complex polytheistic world, delves into the technical aspects of survival, underscoring human agency even in the face of overwhelming divine power. The Genesis account, reflecting a monotheistic worldview, emphasizes God's absolute power and humanity's utter dependence upon divine grace. The flood itself is depicted with less vivid detail in Genesis than in the Gilgamesh epic. While the scale and destructive power are undeniable, the focus remains firmly on God's judgment and the righteous salvation of Noah and his family.

The post-flood narrative in Genesis also differs significantly from its Mesopotamian counterpart. The covenant between God and Noah, symbolized by the rainbow, forms a central theme, highlighting God's promise never again to destroy the earth with a flood. This covenant establishes a new relationship between God and humanity, marked by divine mercy and the promise of continued existence. The emphasis on the covenant establishes a foundational element of the Abrahamic faiths, reflecting a theological perspective absent in the Gilgamesh epic. The post-flood world in Genesis is less a focus on individual survival and more about the establishment of a new order based on God's promise and humanity's renewed responsibility.

Interpretations of the biblical flood narrative have varied widely throughout history. Literal interpretations view the story as a historical account of a global catastrophe, supporting arguments for young-earth creationism and a strict adherence to the biblical text. These literal interpretations often emphasize the divine judgment on humanity's wickedness and the preservation of a righteous remnant. They are frequently tied to specific theological and apologetic projects, seeking to reconcile scientific findings with biblical accounts. Supporting this view, some point to geological evidence of past floods and the seeming impossibility for a global flood to wipe out every species but the ones in the ark.

Conversely, metaphorical interpretations view the flood story as an allegory or parable, conveying deeper theological truths. These interpretations may focus on the themes of divine judgment, repentance, and the promise of redemption.

The flood might symbolize spiritual cleansing, the destruction of sin, or the cyclical nature of creation and destruction. Scholars have suggested that the flood story might be an etiological myth, explaining the origin of the rainbow, the diversity of languages, or the human condition. This approach often seeks to understand the story within its literary and cultural context, recognizing its symbolic power rather than its literal historicity. The metaphorical interpretation allows for a more nuanced engagement with the text, accommodating scientific understandings of the earth's history and embracing the story's symbolic power.

Furthermore, the narrative's influence on subsequent religious and cultural traditions is undeniable. The flood myth has resonated across cultures and time periods, appearing in numerous other religious and literary traditions. These variations demonstrate the enduring power of the deluge archetype to capture the human imagination and express profound concerns about the relationship between humanity and the divine, order and chaos, and creation and destruction. The flood narrative has been used to explain the origins of evil, the existence of suffering, and the persistence of human wickedness. It has also served as a source of inspiration for artistic expression, shaping countless works of literature, art, and music.

Another significant area of interpretation concerns the nature of the flood itself. Was it truly global, encompassing the entire planet, or was it a more localized event, perhaps a catastrophic flood in the Mesopotamian region? This question has fueled much debate among biblical scholars and scientists alike. Arguments for a global flood often center on the interpretation of the Hebrew text, which many interpret as describing a world-wide event. However, geological and archaeological evidence has yet to provide conclusive proof of a worldwide flood of the scale described in Genesis.

Conversely, arguments for a regional flood point to the limitations of ancient geographical knowledge and suggest that the narrative may reflect the experience of a devastating local flood within a more limited area.

The question of the flood's extent is deeply intertwined with the wider discussion of the interpretation of the Bible as a whole. Those who hold to a literal interpretation of scripture tend to argue for a global flood, while those who favor a more nuanced, contextualized reading often lean toward a regional interpretation. This divergence highlights the complex interplay between scientific investigation and theological interpretation, underscoring the challenges of reconciling faith and reason. The scientific method relies on empirical evidence, while religious faith often rests on matters of belief and revelation. Bridging the gap between these two ways of knowing requires thoughtful engagement and a willingness to engage with diverse perspectives.

The ethical implications of the flood narrative also deserve careful consideration. The story can be interpreted as a divine act of judgment against humanity's wickedness, prompting discussions about divine justice, human responsibility, and the nature of sin. Some argue that the flood underscores the importance of righteousness and obedience to God. Others find the narrative problematic, questioning the fairness of a divine punishment that affects innocent people alongside the wicked. Discussions of divine punishment and justice frequently engage with questions of free will, predestination, and the nature of human agency. The story poses difficult questions that challenge us to confront our own beliefs about justice, morality, and the relationship between human actions and divine judgment.

The ongoing relevance of the biblical flood narrative lies in its capacity to explore timeless themes of human fallibility, divine power, and the search for meaning in a complex world. The story continues to resonate with audiences because it grapples with profound questions about morality, justice, and the relationship between humanity and the divine. The narrative's enduring appeal lies in its capacity to confront these questions, even if the answers remain elusive. Its presence in various religious traditions and cultural expressions further solidifies its powerful influence on human understanding and imagination, showcasing its importance as a narrative vehicle for exploring fundamental existential questions that continue to shape human thought and beliefs. The persistent reinterpretation and reimagining of the flood narrative in different eras and cultures underscores its continuing relevance as a potent symbol and a springboard for exploring humanity's relationship with the divine, the natural world, and itself.

Flood Myths in Other Ancient Cultures

The pervasive nature of flood myths across diverse ancient cultures suggests a compelling narrative archetype deeply embedded in the human psyche. While the Mesopotamian and Biblical accounts stand as prominent examples, a closer examination reveals strikingly similar narratives in the annals of other civilizations, provoking questions regarding their origins and transmission. Exploring these parallels offers valuable insights into the shared human experience and the enduring power of myth to address fundamental concerns about creation, destruction, and the relationship between humanity and the divine.

Greek mythology offers a compelling parallel with the deluge myths already discussed. The story of Deucalion and Pyrrha, recounted by Ovid in his *Metamorphoses* , describes a great flood sent by Zeus to punish the wickedness of humanity. Similar to the Mesopotamian and Biblical accounts, this flood is described as a catastrophic event that wipes out almost all of mankind. Deucalion and Pyrrha, however, are spared, guided by the god Prometheus to build an ark, a clear echo of Utnapishtim and Noah's actions. Their survival ensures the continuation of the human race, mirroring the preservation of Noah's family and the repopulation of the earth. While the ark imagery is less central in the Greek narrative, and the flood's divine impetus is less explicitly linked to human wickedness compared to other versions, the essential elements – a global catastrophe, the survival of a righteous couple, and the subsequent repopulation of the earth – are undeniably present. Furthermore, the method of repopulation differs notably. Instead of the direct procreation seen in the Mesopotamian and Biblical narratives, Deucalion and Pyrrha repopulate the earth by throwing stones over their shoulders, which transform into men and women, illustrating a distinct creative process reflecting the specific cultural context of ancient Greece. This variation highlights the adaptive and flexible nature of the flood myth archetype, showcasing its ability to adapt to and reflect specific cultural beliefs and cosmological understandings.

The Egyptian flood narratives, while less centrally focused on a single, world-destroying event like the others, offer intriguing points of comparison. The cyclical inundation of the Nile River, a life-giving force for Egyptian civilization, was deeply interwoven with their religious beliefs and cosmological understanding. The annual flooding was interpreted not as a destructive force, but as a renewal of life and fertility, a process of purification and rebirth associated with Osiris, the god of the underworld and resurrection. The myth of Osiris's death and resurrection, involving his dismemberment and subsequent reassembly by Isis, his sister-wife, reflects the cyclical nature of death and rebirth inherent in the Nile's flooding. Although not a universal deluge, the inundation carried symbolic weight parallel to the great floods described elsewhere. The Nile's inundation, while essential for agriculture, also posed a threat if its intensity or timing was disrupted. This inherent danger mirrored the destructive potential of the universal flood myths, underscoring the vulnerability of human societies to the forces of nature. The connection between the life-giving flood and the cyclical process of death and rebirth in the Osiris myth demonstrates how flood narratives could be reinterpreted to reflect diverse cosmological frameworks.

Moving further East, Hindu mythology presents the story of Manu, a significant figure in Vedic literature. The Matsya Purana relates a story where Manu, a primordial man, is warned by a fish (an avatar of Vishnu) of an impending deluge. Manu is instructed to build a ship and collect pairs of all living beings, including sages and plants. This is strikingly reminiscent of the Noah's Ark narrative, illustrating the remarkable similarities in the plot structure across vastly different geographical and cultural contexts. The fish guides Manu's ship through the turbulent waters, ultimately leading to the rebirth of the world. This narrative emphasizes the divine intervention and guidance crucial to surviving the catastrophic event. The emphasis on the importance of righteousness in Manu's character aligns with the emphasis on piety in Noah's story, although the specific details of this righteousness and divine reward may vary according to each culture's unique values and beliefs. The post-flood world in the Hindu tradition, however, is often portrayed as a period of regeneration and renewal, similar to the Egyptian view of the Nile's inundation, highlighting a shared understanding of the cyclicality of destruction and renewal in nature.

The similarities across these diverse flood narratives, from the Near East to the Indian subcontinent, raise important questions about the origins of this archetype. Did this narrative originate in a single culture and then spread through cultural diffusion, perhaps through trade routes or migratory patterns? Or did similar environmental experiences, like catastrophic floods in different regions, independently give rise to parallel narratives reflecting a common human response to natural disasters? The possibility of independent invention is significant, suggesting a deep-seated human predisposition to create narratives reflecting their fundamental concerns about survival and the power of nature. However, the remarkable structural and thematic similarities between the myths suggest a degree of shared influence, though pinpointing a single origin point remains a complex task hampered by the limitations of the historical record.

The presence of common elements, such as the divine warning, the construction of a vessel for survival, the global or regional scale of the flood, the selection of a righteous individual or group, and the subsequent repopulation of the earth, points towards a strong possibility of at least partial interconnectivity. The variations in details, however, offer crucial insights into the unique cultural values and belief systems that shaped these narratives. For instance, the role of human wickedness in triggering the divine retribution varies across these accounts, reflecting differences in theological perspectives on human nature and the relationship between humanity and the divine. Similarly, the means of repopulation and the nature of the post-flood world often reflect unique cultural values and cosmological understandings, providing valuable clues into the diversity of ancient belief systems.

Furthermore, the continued presence of flood narratives in modern cultures, often adapting and reimagining the original stories, underscores the enduring power and relevance of this archetype. This persistent retelling, reinterpretation, and reimagining demonstrates the flood myth's adaptability and resilience, confirming its significant role in shaping human understandings of the world, the relationship between humanity and the divine, and the cyclical nature of creation and destruction. The flood myth archetype continues to resonate because it provides a framework for grappling with existential questions of mortality, human agency, and the overwhelming power of nature. Through the lens of comparative mythology, we gain a deeper appreciation for the human condition and the enduring power of storytelling in shaping cultural values and beliefs. The consistent presence of the flood myth across diverse cultures and time periods offers a valuable pathway to understanding shared human experiences and the universal quest for meaning in the face of both the mundane and the cataclysmic. The flood, whether a literal event or a symbolic narrative, becomes a powerful metaphor for confronting the fragility of existence and the resilience of the human spirit.

The Symbolic Meaning of the Flood Purification and Renewal

The recurring motif of the flood across diverse mythologies transcends mere narrative coincidence; it functions as a potent symbol, laden with profound implications for understanding the human relationship with the divine and the cyclical nature of existence. Central to this symbolism is the concept of purification, a cleansing process that eradicates the old and prepares the way for the new. In the Mesopotamian flood narrative, the deluge is explicitly presented as divine retribution for the rampant wickedness of humanity. The flood's waters, in this interpretation, act as a purifying agent, washing away the sins and corruption that had permeated the world, leaving behind a cleansed slate upon which a new, more righteous society could be built. This interpretation aligns with the broader Mesopotamian worldview, where ritual purity played a significant role in maintaining cosmic order and ensuring divine favor. The surviving hero, Utnapishtim, is rewarded for his piety and obedience, his survival representing the triumph of righteousness amidst widespread moral decay.

The Biblical flood account echoes this theme of purification, although the emphasis on human wickedness as the primary catalyst is even more pronounced. The story of Noah's Ark depicts God's judgment upon a world steeped in sin and violence, the flood serving as a catastrophic cleansing that wipes away the corrupt and allows for the preservation of a select few deemed worthy of a new beginning. The covenant God establishes with Noah after the flood represents a promise of a reformed relationship between the divine and humanity, a new order built upon a foundation of righteousness and obedience. The rainbow, a prominent symbol in this narrative, serves as a tangible reminder of God's commitment to never again destroy the world through a similar cataclysm. This imagery reinforces the narrative's function not merely as a historical account, but as a powerful theological statement regarding divine justice, mercy, and the promise of redemption.

However, the symbolic significance of the flood isn't exclusively tied to themes of divine punishment and purification from sin. In several traditions, the flood's cleansing power is not solely associated with ethical cleansing, but also with a broader cosmic renewal. This interpretation is particularly evident in the Egyptian understanding of the annual Nile inundation. While not a catastrophic deluge in the same vein as the Mesopotamian or Biblical accounts, the Nile's annual flooding was perceived as a vital process of rejuvenation and fertility. The rising waters, far from being destructive, brought with them the rich silt that nourished the land, ensuring agricultural prosperity and the sustenance of Egyptian civilization. The cyclical nature of the Nile's inundation, mirroring the cycles of death and rebirth, became integral to Egyptian cosmology, deeply intertwined with their understanding of the afterlife and the cyclical nature of creation and destruction. Osiris, the god of the underworld and resurrection, became associated with this renewal, his mythical death and resurrection echoing the transformative power of the floodwaters. The flooding was thus not merely a physical event, but a profound symbolic representation of purification and the ever-recurring cycle of life, death, and rebirth.

The Hindu tradition also offers a nuanced perspective on the symbolic meaning of the flood. In the Matsya Purana, the flood is not presented solely as divine punishment, but also as a necessary process of cosmic cleansing and renewal. The narrative of Manu and the fish (an avatar of Vishnu) emphasizes the importance of divine intervention and guidance in surviving and rebuilding after the catastrophic event. The deluge, in this context, doesn't simply eradicate wickedness; it serves as a catalyst for a new cosmic order, a fresh start that allows for the creation of a more perfect world. This interpretation aligns with the cyclical worldview inherent in Hindu cosmology, where creation and destruction are not seen as opposing forces, but as interconnected aspects of a continuous process of cosmic transformation. The flood, therefore, becomes a symbolic representation of this perpetual cycle, a necessary prelude to the emergence of a new creation.

The symbolism of water itself plays a crucial role in shaping the diverse interpretations of flood narratives. Water, across numerous cultures and belief systems, is often associated with both life and death, creation and destruction, purity and impurity. Its fluidity and transformative power make it a fitting symbol for the cyclical nature of existence, the constant interplay between opposing forces. In many traditions, water is a sacred element, used in purification rituals to cleanse the body and spirit. The flood's waters, therefore, could be interpreted as an amplified version of this ritual cleansing, a massive purification rite enacted on a cosmic scale. The contrast between the life-giving and life-destroying aspects of water adds a layer of complexity to its symbolic meaning, reflecting the duality inherent in the human experience and the forces of nature.

The flood narratives, therefore, offer a rich tapestry of symbolic interpretations. The deluge, whether perceived as divine punishment, cosmic renewal, or a combination of both, serves as a potent metaphor for the human experience. Its association with purification, both ethical and cosmic, emphasizes the cyclical nature of life, death, and rebirth, highlighting the human struggle to maintain order amidst chaos and to find meaning in the face of both catastrophe and renewal. The enduring power of flood myths across cultures and time periods suggests their deep-seated relevance to the human condition. They reflect a fundamental human need to understand and grapple with the unpredictable forces of nature, the ever-present possibility of destruction, and the enduring hope for a new beginning.

Furthermore, the flood narrative's function extends beyond purely symbolic meaning. It also serves as a framework for societal reorganization and the reaffirmation of cultural values. The survivors, often chosen for their piety or righteousness, embody the ideal qualities that the post-flood society should strive to emulate. The narratives, therefore, function as moral guides, reinforcing societal norms and emphasizing the importance of adhering to divine law or cultural values. The rebuilding of society after the flood often represents a deliberate attempt to establish a more just and harmonious social order, reflecting the human desire to create a better world in the aftermath of destruction.

In conclusion, the symbolic meaning of the flood is far richer and more multifaceted than a simple narrative of divine retribution. Across various cultures and religious traditions, it functions as a potent symbol of purification, renewal, and the promise of a new beginning. The symbolism of water, with its inherent duality, further enriches this interpretation, reflecting the complex interplay between life and death, creation and destruction, order and chaos. The consistent recurrence of this archetype highlights the deep-seated human need to make sense of cataclysmic events and to find hope and meaning in the face of overwhelming power. The flood myth, therefore, stands as a powerful testament to the enduring human capacity for both resilience and spiritual reflection, a reflection of the human spirit's ability to emerge renewed and strengthened from even the most catastrophic experiences. It’s a narrative that continues to resonate deeply because it speaks to fundamental human concerns about mortality, survival, and the ongoing search for meaning in a world fraught with both beauty and destruction.

Flood Myths as Reflections of Human Experience

The universality of flood myths across diverse cultures points to a deeper, more fundamental human experience being mirrored in these narratives. While the specific details vary – the divine agent, the method of survival, the reasons for the deluge – the underlying anxieties and hopes remain remarkably consistent. These narratives are not merely stories of cataclysmic events; they are powerful reflections of humanity's enduring struggle to comprehend and cope with the unpredictable forces of nature, the fragility of civilization, and the cyclical nature of life and death.

One prominent theme is the ever-present human anxiety regarding natural disasters. Floods, in their destructive power, represent a potent symbol of the vulnerability of human life in the face of overwhelming natural forces. The sheer scale of destruction depicted in these myths – the obliteration of entire civilizations, the loss of countless lives – speaks directly to the primal human fear of annihilation. This fear is not limited to ancient societies; even in the modern age, with advanced technology and understanding of natural processes, the threat of catastrophic floods continues to haunt populations worldwide. The flood myth, therefore, serves as a timeless expression of this fundamental human anxiety, a way of grappling with the inherent uncertainties and dangers of the natural world.

Beyond the immediate threat of physical destruction, flood myths also often reflect deeper anxieties concerning societal collapse and moral decay. In many versions of the story, the flood is presented as divine retribution for human wickedness, a punishment for widespread sin and corruption. This interpretation suggests that the narrative's function extends beyond a simple explanation of natural phenomena; it also serves as a moral allegory, emphasizing the importance of ethical behavior and social cohesion. The collapse of civilization depicted in the flood myth can be viewed as a symbolic representation of what happens when societal norms and moral values are eroded. The subsequent rebuilding of society after the flood often represents a conscious effort to create a more just and harmonious social order, reflecting humanity's enduring hope for a better future and its capacity for rebuilding after destruction.

The cyclical nature of life and death is another recurring theme powerfully conveyed through the imagery of the flood. The deluge, in many interpretations, is not simply an act of destruction but a process of renewal and rebirth. The waters that destroy also cleanse, washing away the old and creating the conditions for a new beginning. This cyclical pattern aligns with the broader cosmological understanding of many ancient cultures, where creation and destruction are not seen as opposing forces but as interconnected aspects of an ongoing process of cosmic transformation. The flood, therefore, becomes a potent symbol of this perpetual cycle, highlighting the inevitable interplay between life and death, creation and destruction, and the constant renewal that characterizes the natural world and the human experience.

The imagery itself contributes significantly to the enduring power of these myths. The overwhelming force of the floodwaters, the desperate struggle for survival, the subsequent emergence of a new world—these vivid images resonate across cultures and time periods, evoking a range of profound emotional responses. The symbolism of water itself adds another layer of depth. Water, as a life-giving source, is essential for human existence; yet, in its destructive form, it represents the power of nature to obliterate all that it has created. This inherent duality perfectly encapsulates the ambivalent nature of the human relationship with the natural world.

The specific details of the flood narratives differ significantly across cultures, reflecting the unique perspectives and beliefs of each civilization. For example, the Mesopotamian flood story, as recounted in the Epic of Gilgamesh, emphasizes the role of divine retribution for human wickedness. The surviving hero, Utnapishtim, is rewarded for his obedience to the gods, highlighting the importance of piety and adherence to divine commands. In contrast, the Biblical flood narrative focuses on God's covenant with Noah, emphasizing divine mercy and the promise of a new beginning. The rainbow serves as a visual reminder of this covenant, a symbol of God's commitment to never again destroy the world through a global flood.

The Egyptian understanding of the annual Nile inundation, while not a catastrophic deluge in the same sense as the Mesopotamian or Biblical accounts, provides a different perspective on the cyclical nature of life and death. The annual flooding of the Nile was essential for agricultural prosperity, viewed as a life-giving force that brought renewal and fertility. This perspective emphasizes the beneficial aspects of water, highlighting its life-sustaining role in maintaining Egyptian civilization. The cyclical nature of the inundation was integrated into their cosmology, reflecting their belief in the cyclical nature of creation and destruction, death and rebirth.

Similarly, the Hindu flood narrative in the Matsya Purana portrays the flood as a process of cosmic renewal, with the fish avatar of Vishnu guiding Manu to safety and subsequently assisting in the creation of a new world. This narrative highlights the importance of divine intervention and guidance in overcoming the catastrophic event, emphasizing the possibility of survival and the subsequent creation of a better world. The focus here is less on divine punishment and more on cosmic renewal and divine grace.

The common thread woven through these diverse narratives is the fundamental human need to understand and come to terms with the unpredictable forces of nature, the threat of destruction, and the possibility of renewal. The flood myth, in its varied forms, serves as a powerful expression of this deep-seated anxiety and hope. It is a story that continues to resonate with audiences because it speaks to fundamental human concerns about mortality, survival, and the ongoing search for meaning in a world fraught with both beauty and destruction.

Furthermore, these narratives often served as mechanisms for societal restructuring and the reinforcement of cultural values. The survivors, often depicted as pious or righteous individuals, became exemplars for the post-flood society. Their actions and choices shaped the new social order, embodying the ideals that the community should aspire to. The rebuilding process itself represented a conscious effort to establish a more just and equitable society, reflecting the enduring human desire to learn from past mistakes and create a better future. The flood myth, therefore, also functions as a cultural blueprint, outlining the principles of societal reconstruction and moral conduct.

In conclusion, the flood myth transcends its status as a mere narrative; it acts as a profound reflection of the human condition. It encapsulates our anxieties about the unpredictable power of nature, our fears of societal collapse, and our enduring hope for renewal and rebirth. The recurring imagery of water, destruction, and rebirth underscores the cyclical nature of life and the ongoing struggle for meaning and purpose in a world characterized by both devastation and renewal. The diverse interpretations of this archetype across various cultures demonstrate the universality of these concerns and the enduring power of myth to address fundamental human questions about existence, morality, and the search for meaning in the face of chaos and change. The myth's enduring relevance highlights the ongoing human need to make sense of catastrophic events and to find hope amidst uncertainty—a testament to our resilience and our capacity for spiritual and societal renewal.

Ancient Egyptian Beliefs about the Afterlife

The ancient Egyptians held a remarkably nuanced and elaborate belief system surrounding the afterlife, a perspective that profoundly shaped their lives, their rituals, and even their art. Unlike many cultures that viewed death as a definitive end, the Egyptians envisioned a continuation of existence, albeit in a transformed state, in a realm known as the Duat, a shadowy underworld mirroring and contrasting the world of the living. Central to their understanding was the concept of the "ka," often translated as "life force" or "spiritual double," an ethereal twin that remained connected to the physical body. Maintaining the integrity of the ka was paramount, and this was largely achieved through the meticulous process of mummification. The preservation of the body was not merely a matter of hygiene or preservation; it was a crucial act that ensured the continuity of the ka and facilitated its journey to the afterlife. The elaborate rituals surrounding death, far from being morbid observances, were seen as crucial support mechanisms to aid the deceased on this profound voyage.

The journey to the Duat was fraught with challenges, conceived not as a simple transition but as a perilous and complex undertaking. The deceased's soul, or "ba," which was represented as a bird with a human head, embarked on a perilous journey through the underworld, navigating treacherous landscapes and confronting supernatural beings. The ba's success depended on its ability to successfully navigate these trials and ultimately gain admittance to Aaru, the Egyptian paradise, a blissful realm of eternal fields, reminiscent of the fertile lands of the Nile Valley. The imagery of Aaru is consistent with the life-affirming values of Egyptian society, emphasizing the continued cultivation of life even beyond the confines of earthly existence. The contrast between the arduous journey through the Duat and the blissful rewards of Aaru highlights the Egyptian emphasis on the importance of righteous living and the fulfillment of moral obligations. The deceased's actions in life directly determined the outcome of their journey; good deeds paved the path to paradise, while evil acts meant facing eternal punishment.

The Book of the Dead, a collection of spells and incantations compiled over centuries, served as a crucial guide for the deceased navigating this intricate journey. It wasn't a single book but rather a personalized compilation of spells tailored to the individual's circumstances and social standing. Each papyrus scroll was unique, containing a selection of spells and prayers aimed at protecting the deceased from the perils of the Duat and guiding them through the various trials and tribulations. These texts are filled with vivid imagery, magical formulas, and detailed descriptions of the underworld's geography, revealing a profound preoccupation with the mysteries of death and the challenges faced by the soul in its journey to the afterlife. The spells often functioned as a kind of magical protection, warding off harmful spirits and demonic entities that inhabited the Duat. The complexity of the Book of the Dead underscores the detailed and intricate nature of Egyptian beliefs about the afterlife. It demonstrates a society deeply invested in ensuring the successful passage of their deceased loved ones into the next world.

Central to the Egyptian conception of the afterlife was the concept of judgment. Upon arrival in the Duat, the deceased's heart was weighed against the feather of Ma'at, the goddess of truth and justice. This scene, frequently depicted in tomb paintings and the Book of the Dead, vividly portrays the moment of reckoning. The heart, symbolizing the individual's actions and character, was assessed for its purity and moral weight. If the heart proved lighter than the feather, signifying a life lived in accordance with Ma'at's principles, the deceased was deemed worthy of entering Aaru. However, if the heart was heavier, signifying a life marred by wickedness, it would be devoured by Ammut, a monstrous being with the head of a crocodile, the body of a lion, and the hindquarters of a hippopotamus, a powerful symbol of the destructive forces that await those who failed to live virtuously. The judgment scene is not merely a depiction of a judicial process; it is a profound reflection of the Egyptian emphasis on moral accountability and the importance of leading a righteous life.

The ritual of mummification played a critical role in the Egyptian belief system concerning the afterlife. The process itself was meticulously detailed, requiring specialized knowledge and skill. The body was carefully cleaned, embalmed, and wrapped in linen bandages, often adorned with amulets and protective charms. These protective items were believed to safeguard the deceased during their journey to the Duat, protecting them from harm and facilitating their passage through the various trials and obstacles. The intricate process of mummification also extended beyond the physical; it was considered a ritualistic cleansing, preparing the body for its journey to the afterlife. The mummification process was an integral part of their elaborate funerary rituals, aiming to ensure the preservation of the body and the successful passage of the ka and ba into the afterlife. The mummified body served as a dwelling place for the ka, ensuring its survival beyond the earthly realm.

Egyptian mythology offers further insight into their beliefs about the afterlife. Osiris, the god of the underworld and resurrection, played a central role. His myth, involving his murder by his brother Set and his subsequent resurrection, became a powerful symbol of hope and rebirth, offering solace to the Egyptians concerning the inevitability of death. Osiris's resurrection represented the possibility of eternal life, suggesting that even death was not the ultimate end. This myth resonated deeply with the Egyptian belief in the cyclical nature of life and death, mirroring the annual flooding of the Nile and the subsequent renewal of the land. The cycle of death and rebirth became a fundamental metaphor for the human experience, emphasizing the continuing cycle of life and renewal even beyond the grave. Osiris's role as judge of the dead further reinforced the importance of moral conduct and the need to live a righteous life to secure a favorable judgment in the afterlife.

Beyond Osiris, the Egyptians conceived of numerous other deities associated with the underworld and the journey to the afterlife. Anubis, with his jackal head, guided the deceased through the various stages of the funerary process and presided over the mummification. Thoth, the god of wisdom and writing, recorded the judgment of the heart weighing ceremony. These deities were not simply mythological figures; they were active participants in the afterlife, guiding and protecting the deceased in their journey. Their presence throughout the narratives highlights the active involvement of the divine in the process of death and the transition into the other world. The detailed accounts of these deities, their roles, and their interactions with the deceased in the funerary texts are a testament to the rich and complex nature of the Egyptian belief system.

The significance of funerary rituals in the Egyptian context extended beyond mere ceremonial practices; they were integral components of their beliefs about the afterlife, acting as crucial mechanisms to facilitate the journey of the soul. The elaborate preparations for the funeral, the mummification process, the burial rituals, and the offerings presented to the deceased all served specific purposes in ensuring a successful passage into the Duat and ultimately the attainment of eternal life in Aaru. The elaborate tombs, often richly adorned with artwork and provisions, provided a fitting resting place for the deceased and served as a tangible expression of their beliefs about the afterlife. The artwork, depicting scenes from daily life, the journey to the underworld, and the judgment of the heart, offered a visual narrative of the soul's passage and emphasized the importance of living a virtuous life to secure a favorable outcome.

The Egyptian beliefs about the afterlife, therefore, were not simply abstract theological concepts; they were deeply ingrained in the fabric of their society, profoundly shaping their lives, their actions, and their worldview. The emphasis on moral conduct, the meticulous process of mummification, the complex narratives of the underworld, and the elaborate funerary rituals all point to a culture profoundly concerned with the continuation of life beyond death. Their elaborate and well-documented beliefs provide a valuable window into the ancient Egyptian worldview, demonstrating their remarkably complex and sophisticated understanding of the human condition and the mysteries of life and death. The integration of their spiritual beliefs into every facet of their lives underscores the profound significance that the afterlife held for the ancient Egyptians. The enduring fascination with Egyptian mythology and their beliefs about death continues to this day, serving as a testament to their remarkably sophisticated and enduring legacy.

Greek and Roman Conceptions of the Underworld

The vibrant tapestry of ancient religious beliefs extends far beyond the meticulous preparations for the afterlife found in ancient Egypt. Turning our gaze westward, we encounter the strikingly different, yet equally compelling, conceptions of the underworld prevalent in ancient Greece and Rome. While the Egyptians envisioned a complex and often perilous journey through the Duat to reach the paradisiacal Aaru, the Greeks and Romans depicted a more straightforward, albeit equally somber, destination: the underworld ruled by Hades. This realm, far from being a place of elaborate trials and divine judgments as in the Egyptian conception, was generally viewed as a bleak and shadowy kingdom, a reflection of the mortality and transience of earthly existence.

Unlike the Egyptian emphasis on the preservation of the physical body as a vessel for the soul's continued journey, the Greeks and Romans placed less emphasis on physical preservation. While burial rites certainly existed, they were less elaborate and less crucial to the soul's continued existence than the intricate mummification process of the Egyptians. The focus shifted from the physical body to the journey of the soul itself, a journey less arduous and more implicitly determined by one's mortal existence. This is not to say that the Greek and Roman conceptions lacked complexity; rather, their complexity manifested in a different way, emphasizing the psychological and metaphorical aspects of death and the afterlife.

The Greek underworld, ruled by Hades, was a realm of shadows and silence, a stark contrast to the vibrant and active Duat. Hades himself, though powerful, was less of an active participant in the lives of the dead than Osiris in Egyptian mythology. He was more a detached ruler, maintaining order in his kingdom rather than actively judging or guiding the souls within it. Persephone, his queen, holds a pivotal role, reflecting the cyclical nature of life and death through her descent to the underworld and subsequent return to the world of the living. Her story, found in the Homeric Hymns, became a symbol of the changing seasons and the perpetual cycle of growth and decay. Her presence softens the starkness of Hades's realm, suggesting a possible hope for renewal even within the desolate underworld. The myth of Persephone's abduction by Hades also showcases the inherent power imbalances within the mythological narrative, a recurring theme when comparing cross-cultural narratives.

Unlike the carefully orchestrated judgments and trials found in the Egyptian Book of the Dead, the Greek passage to the underworld was generally considered a more straightforward event. The souls simply crossed the river Styx, aided by the ferryman Charon, a figure whose payment was a single obol placed in the mouth of the deceased. This detail reflects the pragmatic nature of Greek beliefs; even in death, there was a need for a transactional exchange, a tangible representation of the importance given to the physical act of passage. The lack of a detailed, individualized judgment, like that of the Egyptians, does not suggest a lack of moral consideration. Instead, the Greeks seemed to have believed that a person's actions in life already determined their fate in the underworld.

The imagery of the Greek underworld is evocative, populated by shadowy figures, including the terrifying Cerberus, the three-headed dog guarding its gates, and the Furies, avengers of wrongdoing. These creatures represent the fears and anxieties surrounding death and the consequences of one's actions, though these were less explicitly tied to a formal judgment system compared to the Egyptians. The Elysian Fields, a region of eternal bliss reserved for heroes and favored mortals, offered a counterpoint to the grimness of the underworld. This paradise, though less extensively detailed than the Egyptian Aaru, served as a hopeful vision of an afterlife rewarded for virtuous deeds. Tartarus, on the other hand, served as a place of eternal punishment for the wicked. It functioned as a counterpart to the Egyptian Ammut, although less visually terrifying. The contrasting images of Elysium and Tartarus mirror the Egyptian dichotomy of Aaru and the judgment of Ammut, indicating a cross-cultural recognition of reward and punishment in the afterlife.

The Roman conception of the underworld, heavily influenced by Greek mythology, incorporated many of the same figures and ideas. However, Roman beliefs often included a greater emphasis on the ancestral spirits and the importance of fulfilling one's familial duties. The Romans placed considerable significance on piety toward the gods and respect for family traditions, and these values extended beyond the realm of the living, significantly influencing their beliefs regarding the afterlife. This suggests a cultural focus more on societal structure and order, which subtly shaped their vision of the underworld. The Underworld’s location, a region of eternal darkness and shadow, maintained the consistent thematic representation across cultures.

The deities associated with the Roman underworld included Pluto (the Roman equivalent of Hades), Proserpina (Persephone), and Dis Pater, a powerful deity associated with the realm of the dead and the agricultural cycle. Similar to their Greek counterparts, these deities held less active roles in the affairs of the deceased compared to the active involvement of Osiris, Anubis, and Thoth in the Egyptian mythology. The emphasis shifted from active participation in the afterlife to the mere existence of a distinct, albeit bleak, realm where souls resided after death. This shift in emphasis reflects a crucial difference in the underlying philosophical views of life and death between the cultures.

While both the Greeks and Romans shared a similar conception of the underworld as a shadowy, subterranean realm, the details and associated myths varied. The Roman emphasis on ancestor veneration provided a unique perspective, blending the religious and social aspects of death. The concept of the Manes, the spirits of the departed ancestors, highlights the importance of family and lineage in Roman culture, impacting their perception of the afterlife in a way that differs from the individualized judgments found in Egyptian beliefs. Rituals involving offerings to these ancestral spirits reveal a deep-rooted cultural belief system where the living and dead maintained a tangible relationship.

In comparing the Greek and Roman conceptions of the underworld with the Egyptian perspective, we uncover fascinating similarities and contrasts. The existence of both paradisiacal and punitive afterlives—Elysium/Aaru and Tartarus/Ammut's judgment—clearly demonstrates a universal human need to reconcile notions of reward and punishment tied to actions in mortal life. However, the nature of the journey, the role of the deities, and the emphasis on the physical versus the spiritual differed greatly. The Egyptian emphasis on elaborate preparation, rituals, and a detailed judgment process stands in stark contrast to the comparatively simpler, more implicitly determined fate of the Greek and Roman souls. These discrepancies highlight the diversity of human belief systems, but also reveal underlying common threads, illustrating humanity's enduring fascination with the mysteries of death and the possibilities of an afterlife. The differences also highlight the influence of specific cultural values on shaping beliefs about the afterlife, showcasing how religious beliefs are inextricably interwoven with the social fabric of a civilization. By exploring these different belief systems, we uncover deeper layers of understanding concerning the human condition and our enduring search for meaning, both in life and in death. The consistent emergence of similar motifs across vastly different cultures suggests fundamental aspects of the human experience concerning mortality and the desire for continued existence in some form.

The Buddhist Concept of Rebirth and Karma

The narratives surrounding death and the afterlife in ancient civilizations reveal a profound human preoccupation with mortality and the possibility of continued existence. While the Egyptians meticulously prepared for a complex journey through the Duat, and the Greeks and Romans envisioned a simpler, albeit shadowy underworld, the Buddhist perspective offers a radically different framework: the cyclical nature of rebirth governed by karma. Unlike the linear journeys toward a singular afterlife found in other traditions, Buddhism posits a continuous cycle of existence, samsara, where death is not an end but a transition to a new life, shaped by the accumulated consequences of past actions.

This concept of rebirth is not a simple reincarnation of the same soul in a new body. Buddhist philosophy, particularly in its Theravada tradition, doesn't posit a permanent, unchanging self (anatman). Instead, it views consciousness as a stream of interconnected moments, a process of continuous becoming. Death marks the dissolution of this current aggregation of physical and mental components, and a new aggregation arises, conditioned by the karmic residue of previous actions. This is not a literal transfer of a soul but rather a continuation of the stream of consciousness, a new manifestation shaped by the ethical and moral trajectory of past lives. The individual's sense of self-continuity is an illusion, a product of clinging to impermanent phenomena.

Karma, the central mechanism driving this cycle, is not simply a system of rewards and punishments but a principle of causality. Every action, thought, and intention, whether conscious or unconscious, generates karmic imprints. These imprints shape future experiences, influencing the circumstances of subsequent rebirths. Positive actions, driven by compassion, generosity, and wisdom, generate positive karma, leading to happier and more fortunate rebirths. Conversely, negative actions—cruelty, greed, ignorance—generate negative karma, resulting in suffering and less fortunate circumstances. It's a profoundly nuanced system, where even seemingly minor acts accumulate to impact future lives. This isn't a simplistic ledger of good and bad deeds but a complex interplay of intention, action, and consequence, stretching across lifetimes.

Unlike some Western religious traditions that offer a potential escape from the cycle of suffering, Buddhism emphasizes the possibility of liberation (Nirvana). Nirvana, however, isn't a place or a state after death but a cessation of the very cycle of rebirth itself. It is the extinguishing of craving and attachment, the realization of the impermanence of all things, and the transcendence of the self-illusion. Achieving Nirvana requires intense self-cultivation, ethical conduct, and the development of wisdom through meditation and mindfulness. The goal isn't simply a better afterlife, but the complete cessation of suffering and the ending of the continuous cycle of birth, death, and rebirth.

The concept of karma extends beyond individual actions to encompass broader social and environmental consequences. The actions of one individual can have far-reaching effects, impacting others across multiple lifetimes. This interconnectedness highlights the importance of compassion and ethical behavior, not only for individual liberation but for the well-being of all beings. The responsibility extends beyond immediate consequences, emphasizing the long-term and widespread impact of choices. This ethical framework differs significantly from the often more localized and immediate consequences found in other religious systems.

The Buddhist understanding of rebirth offers a complex and profound contrast to the linear perspectives of the ancient Egyptian, Greek, and Roman views of the afterlife. While the Egyptian Book of the Dead meticulously outlines a journey through the underworld, culminating in a judgment that determines one's fate in Aaru or annihilation, Buddhism presents a continuous cycle without a final judgment. The meticulous weighing of the heart against the feather of Ma'at is a singular event, determining a single, definitive afterlife. The Buddhist concept, in contrast, lacks such a final judgment, instead integrating the consequences of actions into the very fabric of each subsequent rebirth. Similarly, the Greek and Roman conceptions of Hades and Elysium, though incorporating elements of reward and punishment, operate within a more linear, less cyclical framework than the Buddhist concept of samsara.

The emphasis on the soul's journey in ancient Greece and Rome, even with its variations concerning the location and characteristics of the underworld, lacks the continuous, self-reinforcing mechanism of karma. Charon's ferry across the Styx represents a single passage, a final transition, not a repetition within a cyclical system. Even the Elysian Fields, offering eternal bliss, is a fixed destination, not a stage within a continuous process of becoming. This fundamental difference in perspective profoundly impacts the understanding of morality and ethics. In the Greek and Roman contexts, morality often relates to one's actions in a single lifetime, their standing within the community, and the fulfillment of social obligations. Death then represents a transition to a final state – a destination, rather than a transition point within an ongoing process.

Buddhist karma, however, necessitates a more far-reaching ethical consideration. Actions in one life directly shape the circumstances of subsequent lives, extending the consequences of choices far beyond the span of a single existence. This inherent temporality demands a heightened awareness of one's actions, not just for immediate gratification or avoidance of punishment, but for the long-term impact on one's own continuous existence and the well-being of all sentient beings. It fosters a deeper sense of responsibility and interconnectedness, shifting the focus from individual reward or punishment to collective well-being.

Furthermore, the Buddhist concept challenges the very notion of a fixed self, an unchanging essence that transcends death. The absence of an atman, a permanent soul, radically alters the understanding of identity and continuity. The individual is seen as an ever-changing aggregation of physical and mental phenomena, constantly influenced by karma and shaped by experience. The illusion of a permanent self is a significant factor in the cycle of suffering, as attachment to this illusion perpetuates the cycle of rebirth. The path to liberation involves relinquishing this attachment, accepting the impermanent nature of existence, and cultivating wisdom and compassion.

The detailed afterlife narratives of ancient Egypt, with their elaborate funerary rituals and detailed judgment scenes, stand in sharp contrast to the more implicit and nuanced system of karma and rebirth. The explicit judgments of Osiris and the weighing of the heart create a clear, linear progression, with a defined outcome. Buddhism, however, offers no such final judgment. The consequences of actions are not assessed at a single point, but rather continuously shape and influence each successive rebirth. This subtle yet profound difference highlights the divergence in worldviews and spiritual goals. The Egyptian focus on the preservation of the physical body and the soul's journey through the Duat reveals a concern for preserving individual identity beyond death. Buddhism, in contrast, focuses on transcending the individual self entirely to achieve liberation from the cycle of suffering.

This comparison of different perspectives highlights the remarkable diversity of human approaches to understanding death and the afterlife. Each tradition, shaped by unique cultural and historical contexts, reveals its own distinctive methods for grappling with the profound questions surrounding mortality, the meaning of life, and the possibility of existence beyond death. Yet, despite their differences, these ancient beliefs share a common thread: a profound desire to find meaning and purpose in human existence, to reconcile the experience of mortality with the yearning for continued existence and ultimate well-being. The exploration of these diverse beliefs, therefore, provides valuable insights into the enduring human search for understanding, meaning, and ultimately, liberation from suffering. Whether it's the elaborate preparations for the afterlife in ancient Egypt, the journey to the shadowy underworld in ancient Greece and Rome, or the cyclical rebirth guided by karma in Buddhism, these narratives reveal a profound commonality: the enduring human quest for meaning and transcendence.

Abrahamic Beliefs about Heaven Hell and Judgment

The Abrahamic faiths—Judaism, Christianity, and Islam—share a common ancestor in their belief in a single God and, consequently, exhibit striking similarities in their eschatological views, despite variations in detail and emphasis. Central to their understanding of the afterlife are the concepts of heaven, hell, and a divine judgment that determines an individual's ultimate fate. However, the specifics of these beliefs differ significantly, reflecting the unique historical and theological developments within each tradition.

Judaism, the oldest of the three Abrahamic religions, offers a less developed and more ambiguous vision of the afterlife compared to its later counterparts. While the Hebrew Bible doesn't explicitly detail a heaven or hell in the same way as Christianity or Islam, it does allude to concepts of reward and punishment in the afterlife. The idea of a resurrection, the revival of the dead, is present, though not consistently or universally accepted throughout Jewish history and thought. Instead of a vividly described heaven and hell, early Jewish thought focused on a concept of "Sheol," a shadowy underworld where all souls, regardless of their earthly deeds, ultimately went. Sheol was not a place of eternal torment or reward, but rather a more neutral realm.

Over time, however, Jewish thought evolved to incorporate more nuanced views of the afterlife. Pharisaic Judaism, a significant branch of Judaism during the Second Temple period, introduced a more clearly defined belief in resurrection and the ultimate judgment of God. This belief played a pivotal role in the development of later Abrahamic concepts of heaven and hell. In this view, righteous individuals would experience reward in the afterlife, while the wicked would face divine punishment. This more developed eschatology influenced the later Christian and Islamic understanding of judgment and reward, particularly through the writings of the Second Temple period, influencing the early formulations of Christian and Islamic beliefs.

Christianity, inheriting and building upon Jewish traditions, significantly expands on the afterlife concepts. The New Testament describes heaven as a realm of eternal bliss and communion with God, a place of perfect peace, joy, and unending life. In contrast, hell is presented as a place of eternal suffering and separation from God, a state of torment and despair. The concept of a final judgment, where God assesses the actions of each individual, is crucial to Christian eschatology. Jesus' teachings emphasize the importance of faith, love, and good works as prerequisites for attaining salvation and entering heaven. The Christian conception of salvation often includes the belief in atonement through Christ's sacrifice, which is viewed as a necessary step in reconciliation with God and avoiding eternal damnation.

The Christian concept of resurrection takes a central role in determining one’s destiny. The resurrection of Jesus is seen as a guarantee of the resurrection of believers, ensuring the ultimate triumph over death and the promise of eternal life in heaven. This hope of resurrection profoundly impacted early Christian communities, providing comfort and strength during times of persecution. This concept of a bodily resurrection, a new and glorified existence, distinguishes the Christian understanding of the afterlife from certain other traditions where the focus is on the soul's journey or reincarnation.

The details concerning the nature of heaven and hell, however, have been subject to various interpretations and theological debates within Christianity. Some branches emphasize the literal aspects of heaven and hell, portraying them as physical locations, while others view them more metaphorically, as states of being or relationship with God. This diversity within the Christian faith reflects the complexity and richness of its theological heritage and the enduring struggle to comprehend the mysteries of the afterlife.

Islam, the youngest of the three Abrahamic faiths, incorporates and modifies elements from both Judaism and Christianity in its perspective on the afterlife. Islamic eschatology, detailed in the Quran and Hadith, presents a vivid and detailed description of heaven (Jannah) and hell (Jahannam). Jannah is portrayed as a paradise of unimaginable beauty and pleasure, a garden filled with rivers of milk and honey, where the faithful will reside in eternal bliss. Jahannam, on the other hand, is described as a place of intense fire and suffering, reserved for those who reject God's guidance.

The Day of Judgment (Yawm al-Qiyāmah) plays a central role in Islamic eschatology. God will weigh the good deeds and sins of each individual, determining their ultimate destiny. The balance of good and evil actions directly influences whether one is destined for paradise or hell. Intermediary stages may also occur before the ultimate judgment, reflecting aspects of soul refinement and divine mercy. This emphasis on a judgment day creates a sense of accountability and urgency in Islamic life, inspiring both piety and good works.

Furthermore, Islam shares the belief in bodily resurrection. The deceased will be resurrected on the Day of Judgment to face the divine assessment. This belief strengthens the concept of personal accountability and the impact of earthly actions on one's eternal fate. It is a powerful motivator for ethical living and adherence to God's laws. This concept of a bodily resurrection creates a framework quite different from those encountered in ancient Egyptian beliefs, for example, where the emphasis falls on preserving the body for the afterlife, as well as the Buddhist belief in the impermanence of the self, with no fixed soul surviving death.

While all three Abrahamic faiths share the core beliefs in heaven, hell, and divine judgment, the specifics of these beliefs vary. The extent of detail in the descriptions, the emphasis on different aspects of the afterlife, and even the precise nature of heaven and hell are all open to interpretation and debate within each tradition. These differences stem from different historical contexts, theological interpretations, and the unique emphasis each faith places on certain aspects of divine revelation and human experience.

Despite these variations, the common thread is a profound belief in divine justice and the ultimate accountability of human actions. This shared emphasis on judgment reinforces the importance of ethical living and the belief that one's choices in life have eternal consequences. The hope of heaven and the fear of hell both serve as powerful incentives for believers to strive for righteousness and piety, ensuring the Abrahamic eschatology plays a pivotal role in shaping the religious lives and ethics of their adherents. The parallels and divergences in their conceptions of the afterlife provide a fascinating window into the evolution of religious thought, revealing how core beliefs adapt and are redefined across different times and cultural contexts. The study of these distinct yet interconnected systems offers a rich understanding of the human experience and the persistent search for meaning and purpose beyond the confines of mortality.

Common Themes in Afterlife Beliefs The Human Search for Meaning Beyond Death

The preceding chapters have explored a diverse range of afterlife beliefs, from the elaborate funerary rituals of ancient Egypt to the nuanced eschatology of the Abrahamic faiths. While the specific details vary dramatically across cultures and time periods, a closer examination reveals striking commonalities, suggesting a fundamental human preoccupation with the possibility of life beyond death. This shared concern transcends geographical boundaries, cultural differences, and even vastly disparate theological frameworks. The quest to understand what happens after death appears to be a universal human experience, reflected in the widespread existence of afterlife beliefs across diverse societies throughout history.

One of the most prevalent themes is the concept of judgment. Whether it's the weighing of the heart against the feather of Ma'at in ancient Egyptian mythology, the divine judgment of Osiris, or the Day of Judgment in Abrahamic faiths, the idea of a final reckoning is remarkably consistent. This suggests a deeply ingrained human sense of justice, a belief that actions have consequences, extending beyond the mortal realm. This belief in accountability, often linked to a higher power or divine force, provides a moral framework and a sense of purpose within earthly life. The anticipation of a judgment, whether positive or negative, shapes behavior and motivates ethical conduct, underscoring the pervasive influence of afterlife beliefs on human morality. Even in cultures where the emphasis is less on a specific judgment day, the concept of karmic consequences, as seen in various Eastern religions, serves a similar purpose, suggesting a form of cosmic justice inherent in the universe itself.

Closely related to the concept of judgment is the notion of reward and punishment. The promise of reward in the afterlife – be it eternal bliss in a heavenly paradise, reincarnation into a higher state of being, or reunion with loved ones – serves as a powerful incentive for righteous living and adherence to religious principles. Conversely, the threat of punishment – whether it be eternal damnation in hell, rebirth into a lower state, or continued suffering in a shadowy underworld – discourages wrongdoing and reinforces societal norms. This duality, the promise of reward juxtaposed with the threat of punishment, is a recurring motif in afterlife beliefs worldwide, suggesting a profound human need for both hope and fear as motivators for ethical behavior and adherence to the moral codes of specific cultures. The interplay of these positive and negative incentives forms a powerful influence on religious practice and societal morality.

Another pervasive theme is the concept of a journey to the otherworld. Whether it's traversing the perilous underworld of Greek mythology, navigating the Duat in ancient Egyptian beliefs, or ascending to the heavens in various Abrahamic traditions, the journey itself often becomes a significant element of the afterlife narrative. These journeys are often fraught with challenges, trials, and symbolic obstacles that the deceased must overcome, often with assistance from divine figures, guides, or the help of sacred texts. The metaphorical nature of this journey suggests a deeper human understanding of death as a transition, a passage from one state of being to another. The symbolism embedded in these journeys reflects the human struggle to make sense of the unknown and find a path through the ambiguity of death. The obstacles encountered, from demonic beings to trials of judgment, often symbolize the internal struggles and challenges faced in life and the importance of ethical behavior to succeed in the transition to the afterlife.

The belief in an intermediary state between life and the ultimate afterlife is also common across various traditions. Examples include the ancient Egyptian concept of the Duat, the Buddhist concept of bardo, and the various purgatorial states described in some Christian traditions. This intermediary state often involves a period of assessment, purification, or preparation before the soul reaches its final destination. The existence of such transitional states points to the human desire for a less abrupt transition between life and death, a period of reconciliation, cleansing, or preparation for the unknown that lies beyond. This liminal phase can be viewed as a period of reflection, a time for the soul to learn from its past experiences and prepare for its ultimate fate.

Furthermore, the role of intermediaries and guides in the afterlife journey frequently appears across cultures. Whether it's the ancient Egyptian psychopomp Anubis, the Greek Hermes, or various angelic beings in Abrahamic faiths, these figures assist the deceased in navigating the complexities of the transition. These intermediaries often embody the transition from the mortal world to the afterlife, assisting in the transformation of the soul and guiding the deceased to their final resting place. They represent hope and guidance in a time of uncertainty, emphasizing the human need for support and comfort in the face of the unknown.

Finally, the enduring human desire for continuity and connection beyond death is a powerful force shaping afterlife beliefs. The hope for reunion with loved ones, the preservation of personal identity, and the continuation of one's essence in some form after physical death are recurring themes across different religious traditions. This desire manifests in various ways, from the Egyptian practice of mummification and the offering of funerary goods to the Christian belief in resurrection and the Islamic belief in bodily resurrection and the reunion of loved ones in paradise. The need for continuity serves as the emotional core of many afterlife beliefs, providing a source of comfort and solace in the face of mortality.

In conclusion, while the details of afterlife beliefs are remarkably diverse, a core set of common themes emerges. The concepts of judgment, reward and punishment, a journey to the otherworld, intermediary states, spiritual guides, and the longing for continuity beyond death demonstrate a universality in the human experience of mortality and the search for meaning beyond it. These recurring motifs suggest that the human fascination with the afterlife is not merely a cultural construct, but a deep-seated psychological and spiritual impulse—a reflection of our fundamental need to understand our place in the universe, grapple with our own mortality, and find hope amidst the uncertainties of life and death. The study of these beliefs allows us to understand not just the history of religion, but the enduring human quest for meaning and purpose.

Gilgamesh The Epic Hero and his Quest for Immortality

The Epic of Gilgamesh, originating in ancient Mesopotamia, offers a compelling exploration of the human condition, particularly the yearning for immortality. Unlike many later heroic narratives where immortality is often a divinely granted reward, Gilgamesh's pursuit is a deeply personal and ultimately tragic quest, shaped by his flaws and the limitations of his mortal existence. He is a king, two-thirds god and one-third human, a powerful figure ruling over Uruk, yet his very divinity underscores the fragility of his mortal coil. This inherent contradiction fuels his desperate search for eternal life, a search that forces him to confront his own mortality and, in doing so, to achieve a form of immortality far different from what he initially envisioned.

Gilgamesh's initial character is defined by his arrogance and self-centeredness. He is depicted as a tyrannical ruler, abusing his power and exploiting his subjects. His strength is legendary, but his actions reflect a profound lack of empathy and understanding. His relentless pursuit of pleasure and his disregard for the consequences of his actions set the stage for his transformative journey. The epic does not portray him as inherently evil, but rather as a flawed character whose flaws are magnified by his immense power and his divine heritage. This initial portrayal establishes a clear contrast between his early reign of terror and his eventual acceptance of his mortality and the responsibilities that come with it. The narrative masterfully uses this contrast to highlight the potential for human growth and transformation.

The death of Enkidu, Gilgamesh's closest friend, serves as the pivotal catalyst in Gilgamesh's quest for immortality.

Enkidu, a wild man tamed by Gilgamesh, represents a crucial counterbalance to the king's arrogant self-assurance. Their friendship is a complex and nuanced relationship, marked by both fierce loyalty and heated disagreements. Enkidu's death, therefore, is not merely a plot device; it triggers a profound existential crisis within Gilgamesh, forcing him to confront the inevitability of his own demise. The visceral nature of Enkidu's death, described in graphic detail, underscores the brutal reality of mortality and the profound grief that accompanies loss. This loss shatters Gilgamesh's self-perception, exposing the emptiness of his earlier pursuits of power and pleasure.

Driven by his grief and terror of his own mortality, Gilgamesh embarks on his arduous quest for immortality. He seeks out Utnapishtim, the only mortal granted immortality by the gods. This journey itself is a significant part of the epic, depicting a series of trials and challenges that Gilgamesh must overcome. He faces physical hardships, traversing treacherous landscapes and enduring unimaginable fatigue. But beyond the physical challenges, the journey also represents an internal transformation. He confronts his own limitations, both physical and emotional, recognizing the shortcomings of his previous life and the need for self-reflection and change. The journey itself is a microcosm of the human struggle against mortality, mirroring the trials and tribulations faced by humanity in its quest for meaning and purpose.

His journey takes him to the Cedar Forest, where he battles the monstrous Humbaba, a guardian of the forest. This encounter is not merely a test of physical strength; it also symbolizes Gilgamesh's struggle with his inner demons – his arrogance and his fear of death. The defeat of Humbaba signifies a victory, not just over a monstrous creature, but over his own internal struggle with his mortality. The acquisition of the cedar wood, a symbol of power and immortality, is a tangible representation of his initial ambition, but it fails to bring him the immortality he so desperately seeks. The epic cleverly demonstrates the fallacy of acquiring material possessions as a means to achieve a transcendental goal.

Upon reaching Utnapishtim, Gilgamesh is presented with the opportunity to gain immortality through a test of endurance. The test, however, is not one of physical strength but rather of self-control and acceptance. Utnapishtim challenges Gilgamesh to stay awake for six days and seven nights, a feat that symbolizes the difficulty of confronting the realities of life and death. Gilgamesh fails the test, demonstrating the limitations of human endurance and his inability to conquer the inevitable. This failure, however, is not presented as a complete defeat. The narrative highlights the limitations of human capabilities in the face of divine power while emphasizing the significance of human striving. Gilgamesh's failure to achieve immortality by supernatural means, instead, leads him to a different kind of immortality.

Despite his failure to achieve physical immortality, Gilgamesh's journey fundamentally changes him. He returns to Uruk a changed man, having shed his arrogance and embraced humility. He no longer seeks immortality through supernatural means but instead finds a form of lasting significance in his responsibilities as a king and his relationship with his people. He understands that true immortality, while not everlasting life, is found in the legacy one leaves behind, in the impact one makes on the lives of others, and in the enduring power of human connection. This transformation is a cornerstone of the epic's enduring power – showcasing the possibility of growth, self-discovery, and the acceptance of mortality as a defining element of human existence.

The Epic of Gilgamesh doesn't merely offer a straightforward adventure story; it delves into complex philosophical themes regarding the nature of humanity, mortality, and the search for meaning. The narrative challenges the very concept of immortality, suggesting that true immortality might lie not in defying death but in embracing life fully, acknowledging its limitations, and leaving a positive mark on the world. This nuanced exploration of mortality and the human condition is what distinguishes the Epic of Gilgamesh from many other heroic narratives. The epic's enduring appeal stems from its profound understanding of human nature and its timeless exploration of existential questions that resonate with readers across cultures and generations.

The quest for immortality in the Epic of Gilgamesh is not a simple pursuit of an external prize. It becomes a deeply introspective journey, leading to Gilgamesh's acceptance of his mortality and a re-evaluation of his values. This journey illustrates that true growth and meaning may often be found not in achieving one's initial ambition, but in overcoming the obstacles and challenges that arise along the way. Gilgamesh's transformation highlights the importance of facing the realities of life and death, of accepting one’s limitations, and recognizing the profound impact of human relationships in defining our existence.

The symbolism woven throughout the narrative further enriches its message. The Cedar Forest, with its monstrous guardian Humbaba, represents the challenges and obstacles encountered in life's journey, both external and internal. The plant of immortality, offered by Utnapishtim, symbolizes the elusive nature of true immortality and the potential for disappointment when chasing unattainable goals. The snake stealing the plant signifies the inevitability of death, a stark reminder of the limitations of human existence. This complex tapestry of symbolism elevates the narrative beyond a mere adventure story, granting it a deeper philosophical and psychological dimension.

In essence, the Epic of Gilgamesh's exploration of immortality transcends the purely physical. The tale serves as a powerful allegory for the human condition, reminding us that while physical mortality is inescapable, the impact we have on the world and the connections we forge can endure beyond our mortal lives. The epic's enduring legacy is a testament to its ability to explore universal themes of loss, grief, friendship, and the ongoing human quest for meaning in a world where death is an inescapable reality. Gilgamesh's journey, though ultimately unsuccessful in achieving immortality in the literal sense, achieves a far greater significance: the story itself achieves a form of immortality through its continued resonance with readers and its exploration of enduringly relevant human experiences. The epic's enduring relevance lies in its ability to tap into the fundamental human desire for meaning, purpose, and lasting legacy in the face of mortality. This resonating truth is arguably a form of immortality itself.

Heracles Hercules and the Twelve Labors

Heracles, the Greek hero known to the Romans as Hercules, stands as a compelling figure in the pantheon of mythological heroes, his legend echoing across centuries and cultures. While the Epic of Gilgamesh explores the quest for immortality through a deeply personal and ultimately tragic journey, Heracles' narrative focuses on the triumph of strength, courage, and perseverance in the face of seemingly insurmountable challenges. His twelve labors, meticulously documented in various ancient Greek texts, serve as a rich tapestry of archetypal themes and symbolic narratives that resonate with the human experience of overcoming adversity. Unlike Gilgamesh's introspective search for immortality, Heracles' journey is outwardly focused, a series of physical and psychological trials imposed as penance for his past actions, yet ultimately shaping him into a paragon of heroic virtue.

The very conception of Heracles is steeped in mythology. The son of Zeus, king of the gods, and Alcmene, a mortal woman, his birth itself is marked by divine intervention and foreshadows his exceptional destiny. Hera, Zeus's jealous wife, harasses Heracles throughout his life, a constant obstacle mirroring the challenges individuals often face in pursuing their goals. This divine interference adds another layer of complexity to Heracles' narrative, differentiating it from Gilgamesh's more self-driven quest. Hera's actions represent external forces that obstruct Heracles' path, highlighting the external pressures that often accompany the pursuit of greatness.

The twelve labors themselves are remarkable for their diversity and their symbolic significance. They are not simply a list of feats of strength; each task presents a unique set of obstacles, both physical and psychological, requiring Heracles to utilize not only his legendary strength but also his cunning, intelligence, and resourcefulness. For example, his first labor, the slaying of the Nemean Lion, highlights his raw strength and his ability to overcome seemingly indestructible foes. The lion's hide, impenetrable to conventional weapons, becomes a symbol of Heracles' own invulnerability, a tangible representation of his triumph over seemingly impossible odds.

The second labor, the slaying of the Lernaean Hydra, presents a more complex challenge. The Hydra, a multi-headed serpent, regenerates two heads for every one severed, demanding not just brute force but strategic thinking. This labor symbolizes Heracles' capacity for problem-solving and adaptation. His use of fire to cauterize the wounds prevents regeneration, indicating his intelligent approach to overcoming seemingly impossible odds. This labor underlines the importance of not just physical strength, but also mental agility and preparedness to counter adversity. It’s a striking contrast to Gilgamesh's reliance on divine assistance or the help of companions; Heracles, for the most part, relies on his own wits and physical prowess.

Further emphasizing the multifaceted nature of Heracles' heroism, the third labor, the capture of the Erymanthian Boar, showcases his hunting skills and mastery over the natural world. This task requires Heracles not only to subdue a wild beast but also to navigate treacherous terrain, demonstrating his resourcefulness and his connection to nature. His ability to skillfully trap and subdue the boar underscores his capacity to harness his skills and knowledge to achieve his objectives. The capture of the boar is not merely a display of strength; it represents Heracles' command over his environment and his ability to use strategy and cunning to overcome challenges.

The cleansing of the Augean stables, Heracles' fifth labor, represents a different kind of challenge. This task required Heracles to clean the enormous stables of King Augeas, a task deemed impossible due to the accumulated manure of thirty years. The solution, however, is not brute force, but ingenuity. Heracles redirects two rivers to wash away the filth, demonstrating not only his understanding of the natural world but also his inventiveness in finding unconventional solutions. This showcases his capability of thinking outside the box and utilizing his knowledge of the natural world. Unlike Gilgamesh's physical battles, Heracles' labors often involve a combination of physical strength and intelligent strategy.

In contrast to Gilgamesh's quest for immortality, Heracles' labors are a form of atonement, a means to redeem himself for past transgressions. While Gilgamesh's journey is driven by a personal desire, Heracles' is imposed by a higher authority, Eurystheus, the king of Mycenae. This external imposition adds a layer of external pressure absent in Gilgamesh's self-imposed quest. While Gilgamesh's journey is a search for self-discovery, Heracles' emphasizes the importance of fulfilling one's obligations and facing the consequences of one's actions. This aspect introduces the concept of duty and societal responsibility, a theme largely absent in the Epic of Gilgamesh.

The abduction of the Cattle of Geryon (tenth labor) presents a challenge that extends beyond physical strength into the realm of deception and trickery. Geryon, a monstrous three-bodied creature, is a formidable opponent. Heracles' success in this labor is not solely due to his strength, but his ability to outsmart his adversary, utilizing cunning and strategic thinking to overcome a formidable opponent. This reinforces his versatility as a hero, capable of adapting his approach to meet the demands of different challenges. This labor displays a different dimension of his heroism, moving beyond brute force into the realm of intelligence and calculated action.

The capture of Cerberus (twelfth labor), the three-headed hound guarding the gates of the Underworld, stands as the ultimate test. This labor transcends the physical realm and enters the symbolic domain of death and the afterlife. Heracles' ability to subdue Cerberus, a creature associated with death itself, solidifies his status as a hero capable of conquering even the most profound fears and confronting mortality itself. This labor provides a direct contrast to Gilgamesh's grappling with mortality; while Gilgamesh seeks to overcome death, Heracles confronts it directly, proving his dominance even over the forces of the underworld.

Each labor, therefore, is a microcosm of the human struggle against adversity. They are not simply feats of strength, but symbolic representations of the challenges individuals face throughout life – challenges that demand courage, perseverance, resilience, and a capacity for adaptation. Heracles' success in each labor is not just a demonstration of his physical capabilities, but a testament to the power of the human spirit to overcome obstacles and achieve greatness. His twelve labors offer a powerful and enduring narrative that inspires and resonates across cultures, demonstrating the power of perseverance, adaptability, and the triumph of the human spirit in the face of adversity.

In comparing Heracles to Gilgamesh, we see a fascinating dichotomy. Gilgamesh's quest is inward-focused, a deeply personal struggle with mortality and self-discovery. Heracles' journey, on the other hand, is outward-focused, a series of trials that serve as a testament to his strength, resilience, and the ultimate triumph of good over evil. Both heroes, however, ultimately achieve a form of immortality, though in vastly different ways. Gilgamesh finds a form of immortality in his legacy, in the impact he leaves on the world, and in the enduring power of his story. Heracles achieves immortality through his legendary deeds, which continue to inspire and resonate across time and cultures. Both narratives demonstrate that true immortality lies not merely in physical existence, but in the enduring legacy one leaves behind and the impact one has on the world.

The enduring appeal of both Heracles and Gilgamesh lies in their ability to represent fundamental aspects of the human condition. The challenges they face, both internal and external, resonate with the struggles of humanity across time and cultures. The heroic qualities they display – strength, courage, perseverance, and intelligence – remain inspiring ideals that continue to capture the imagination of audiences. Their stories transcend their specific cultural contexts, serving as powerful allegories of the human experience and the enduring quest for meaning and purpose in the face of life's inevitable challenges.

The common thread linking both Gilgamesh and Heracles is the idea of a transformative journey. Gilgamesh's journey leads him to a profound understanding of mortality and the importance of human relationships. Heracles' journey transforms him from a figure marred by his past actions into a symbol of heroic virtue and the potential for redemption. Both narratives offer profound insights into the complexities of the human experience, highlighting the transformative potential of adversity and the capacity for personal growth in the face of overwhelming odds. The parallels between these two heroes, despite their different cultural backgrounds and the nature of their respective quests, offer a compelling case study in the universality of archetypal themes in mythology and the enduring human fascination with stories of heroes and their triumphs over adversity. The different approaches, however – Gilgamesh's introspective quest versus Heracles' externally imposed labors – highlight the diverse paths to achieving self-realization and leaving a lasting legacy.

The Buddhas Enlightenment and his Path to Nirvana

The narratives of Gilgamesh and Heracles, while profoundly different in their specific details, both illuminate the human quest for meaning and purpose, a quest often framed within the context of overcoming seemingly insurmountable obstacles. This yearning for transcendence, for a state beyond the limitations of ordinary human experience, finds a powerful articulation in the life and teachings of Siddhartha Gautama, the historical Buddha. Unlike the explicitly heroic narratives of Gilgamesh and Heracles, the Buddha’s path to enlightenment presents a different, yet equally compelling, model of heroism – one focused on inner transformation rather than external feats of strength. His journey, however, is no less arduous, and the challenges he confronts are no less significant.

Siddhartha Gautama's life, as recounted in various Buddhist scriptures, begins within the privileged confines of a royal palace, sheltered from the harsh realities of suffering. His father, King Suddhodana, shielded him from the realities of sickness, old age, and death, hoping to secure his son's future as a powerful ruler. However, fate, or perhaps Siddhartha's own inherent inclination toward spiritual seeking, intervened. Through encounters with an old man, a sick man, and a corpse, Siddhartha was confronted, for the first time, with the inescapable realities of the human condition – the inevitability of decay, disease, and death. This shattering encounter shook him to his core, revealing the ephemeral nature of earthly existence and the pervasiveness of suffering. This profound awareness sparked a pivotal moment in his life, compelling him to abandon his privileged life and embark on a spiritual quest to understand and overcome the suffering he had witnessed.

This decision marks the beginning of Siddhartha's heroic journey, a journey inward rather than outward. His renunciation of princely life, a sacrifice of comfort and security for the uncertain path of spiritual seeking, acts as a powerful statement of his commitment to finding a solution to the pervasive suffering he had observed. This act of renunciation itself is an embodiment of a distinct kind of heroism, one that prioritizes spiritual liberation over material gain, and inner transformation over external achievement. This contrasts sharply with the externally focused heroism of Heracles, whose labors were imposed upon him, and Gilgamesh, whose quest was propelled by a desire for immortality and recognition. The Buddha's heroism lies in his unwavering determination to overcome suffering, not through brute force or heroic deeds, but through self-discipline, introspection, and the cultivation of wisdom.

His quest led him to encounter various ascetics and spiritual teachers, seeking guidance and understanding. He embraced extreme ascetic practices, pushing his body to the limits of endurance in a desperate attempt to extinguish suffering. However, he soon realized that this path, characterized by self-mortification and deprivation, was not the answer. This realization underscores the importance of balance and moderation in the Buddhist path; the extremes of asceticism did not lead to enlightenment but rather to physical and mental exhaustion, revealing the limitations of such a purely physical approach to spiritual liberation.

The turning point in the Buddha's journey came with his rejection of extreme asceticism and his adoption of the "Middle Way." This middle path, avoiding both self-indulgence and self-mortification, became the cornerstone of his teachings. This conscious choice to adopt a balanced and moderate approach underscores the wisdom and adaptability that characterizes his heroic journey. Unlike the unwavering, sometimes even reckless, pursuit of their goals by Gilgamesh and Heracles, the Buddha's path is marked by reflection, self-awareness, and a capacity for reassessment. His willingness to abandon a path that proved unproductive, even after great personal sacrifice, demonstrates a remarkable degree of intellectual humility and a commitment to finding the most effective means to achieve enlightenment.

His enlightenment, achieved under the Bodhi tree, is not a singular event, but the culmination of years of rigorous self-discipline, meditation, and profound reflection. This enlightenment is not a sudden revelation, but a gradual unfolding of wisdom, a profound understanding of the nature of reality and the cessation of suffering. The enlightenment experience itself, while described in various Buddhist texts, remains deeply personal and arguably ineffable, defying simple explanation or categorization. Nevertheless, its essence is a profound transformation, a shift in consciousness that frees the Buddha from the cycle of birth, death, and rebirth (samsara).

The Buddha's path to enlightenment, therefore, can be seen as a heroic journey of self-discovery, a quest for liberation from the cycle of suffering. His heroism is not manifest in feats of physical strength or external accomplishments, but in his unwavering commitment to understanding and overcoming suffering, his willingness to abandon unproductive paths, his adoption of the Middle Way, and his ultimate attainment of enlightenment. This type of heroism emphasizes inner transformation, self-mastery, and the cultivation of wisdom as the means to achieving liberation, thereby offering a profound contrast to the more outwardly focused heroism of Gilgamesh and Heracles.

Upon achieving enlightenment, the Buddha chose to share his insights, initiating a spiritual revolution that transcended geographical and cultural boundaries. He taught the Four Noble Truths, which articulate the nature of suffering, its origin, its cessation, and the path to its cessation. The Eightfold Path, comprising right understanding, right thought, right speech, right action, right livelihood, right effort, right mindfulness, and right concentration, provides a practical framework for attaining liberation from suffering.

The Buddha's teachings emphasize the importance of ethical conduct, mental discipline, and wisdom. These principles, unlike the often violent and sometimes morally ambiguous actions of Gilgamesh and Heracles, form the foundation of a path towards inner peace and liberation. The emphasis on compassion, non-violence, and the cultivation of loving-kindness further distinguishes the Buddhist model of heroism from the more outwardly aggressive models found in other heroic narratives. The Buddha's heroism lies in his ability to transcend the limitations of his own suffering and offer a path towards liberation for all beings.

The Buddhist concept of Nirvana, the ultimate goal of the Buddhist path, represents a state of liberation from suffering and the cycle of rebirth. It is not simply a heaven or an afterlife, but a state of being characterized by peace, tranquility, and freedom from the limitations of the ego. The attainment of Nirvana, therefore, is the culmination of the Buddha's heroic journey, a testament to the power of self-discipline, wisdom, and compassion. The contrast between the Buddha’s pursuit of Nirvana and the quests of Gilgamesh and Heracles, who sought physical immortality, highlights the different conceptions of immortality – one focused on a state of being beyond the cycle of suffering, the other on prolonging physical existence.

The enduring appeal of the Buddha's story lies in its universal relevance. His struggles with suffering, his exploration of different spiritual paths, his eventual attainment of enlightenment, and his selfless dedication to sharing his wisdom resonate with the human experience across cultures and time periods. The Buddha's narrative offers a powerful and enduring message of hope, a testament to the human capacity for transformation and the possibility of overcoming suffering through self-awareness, self-discipline, and the cultivation of wisdom. His path to enlightenment serves as a powerful counterpoint to the more overtly heroic narratives of Gilgamesh and Heracles, highlighting the diversity of ways in which humans strive for meaning, purpose, and transcendence. The different approaches underscore the multifaceted nature of the human quest for something beyond the limitations of ordinary existence, whether that be immortality, heroic glory, or the liberation from suffering. The common thread is the deeply human desire for something more.

Moses and the Exodus A Narrative of Liberation

The narrative of Moses and the Exodus, as recounted in the Book of Exodus, presents a compelling archetype of liberation, mirroring and contrasting with the heroic journeys explored earlier. While Gilgamesh sought immortality, Heracles sought glory through physical feats, and the Buddha pursued inner peace, Moses's journey centers on the liberation of an entire people from bondage. This liberation is not achieved through individual strength or ascetic practices but through divine intervention and inspired leadership. This makes the Exodus story a unique contribution to the tapestry of ancient hero myths, emphasizing the power of faith and divine agency in the face of seemingly insurmountable odds.

The story begins with the Israelites enslaved in Egypt, a period of profound suffering and oppression. Their plight, depicted in vivid detail in Exodus, serves as a powerful symbol of human vulnerability and the potential for tyranny. The Israelites' enslavement is not merely physical; it is a systematic stripping of their identity and freedom. They are forced into harsh labor, denied their basic human rights, and subjected to the arbitrary power of their Egyptian overlords. This depiction of systematic oppression underscores the moral stakes involved in the Exodus narrative and serves as a powerful reminder of the injustices that can occur when unchecked power is wielded.

Moses, the chosen leader, is initially portrayed as hesitant and self-doubting. God's call to lead the Israelites out of Egypt is not met with immediate acceptance. Moses's objections, detailed in the biblical account, reflect both his humility and his awareness of the seemingly impossible task before him. His reluctance highlights the immense weight of responsibility associated with leadership, particularly in the face of a powerful and oppressive regime. His struggles with self-doubt also contribute to his humanity and relatability, making his eventual triumph all the more inspiring.

God's intervention is not a singular event but a series of miraculous acts designed to both convince Moses and overcome the obstacles imposed by the Pharaoh. The plagues, each a devastating blow to the Egyptian power structure, are described with graphic detail, emphasizing the divine power at play. The plagues are not merely acts of destruction but carefully orchestrated events designed to demonstrate God's power to Pharaoh and persuade him to release the Israelites. Each plague, from the turning of the Nile into blood to the death of the firstborn, serves as a dramatic demonstration of divine power, gradually escalating the pressure on Pharaoh and highlighting the consequences of resistance to God's will.

The parting of the Red Sea is perhaps the most iconic event in the Exodus narrative, a truly miraculous feat that represents the ultimate triumph of divine intervention over human power. The sea splitting to allow the Israelites to pass through and then crashing down on the pursuing Egyptian army is a powerful image that has resonated throughout history. The narrative not only recounts a miraculous event but also underscores the symbolic significance of liberation—a passage from slavery to freedom, from death to life. The parting of the Red Sea becomes a powerful metaphor for the overcoming of seemingly insurmountable obstacles and the ultimate triumph of faith and divine power. This miraculous event solidifies Moses’s role as a divinely appointed leader, reinforcing his authority and inspiring faith amongst the Israelites.

Moses's leadership, however, goes beyond simply leading the Israelites out of Egypt. His role encompasses guiding them through the wilderness, providing spiritual and moral guidance, and establishing a covenant between God and his people. The receiving of the Ten Commandments atop Mount Sinai represents a pivotal moment in the narrative, establishing a set of moral and ethical principles that would shape the Israelites' identity and future. These commandments, far from being arbitrary rules, form the foundation of a just and equitable society. They are a testament to God's concern not only for the liberation of the Israelites but also for the creation of a just and moral community.

The journey through the wilderness is itself a crucial aspect of the narrative. It is not a simple escape but a period of trial and testing, a time during which the Israelites' faith and obedience are repeatedly challenged. The wilderness acts as a crucible, forging the Israelites' identity as a chosen people bound by a covenant with God. The challenges faced during this journey—the scarcity of food and water, the murmurings of discontent, and the constant threat of enemies—emphasize the resilience and endurance required for liberation and the importance of faith in the face of adversity. These challenges also highlight the crucial role of leadership in navigating crisis and maintaining hope during difficult times.

The giving of the manna and the provision of water from the rock are further examples of divine intervention, providing for the Israelites' physical needs and demonstrating God's unwavering commitment to their well-being. These events reinforce the Israelites' faith and underscore the providential nature of their journey. They act as tangible signs of divine grace and support, strengthening their resolve and bolstering their confidence in Moses' leadership. The provision of manna, a miraculous food source, and water from the rock, are powerful symbols of divine sustenance and protection during their arduous journey.

The Exodus narrative, therefore, goes beyond a simple tale of liberation. It is a complex and nuanced story that explores themes of divine intervention, leadership, faith, obedience, and the creation of a moral community. Moses's leadership is not based solely on his own strength or ability but on his connection to the divine and his capacity to inspire faith and obedience in his people. The narrative consistently emphasizes the power of God's intervention in shaping the course of events and providing the necessary support for the Israelites' survival and liberation. The Israelites' journey through the wilderness is not a passive experience but a dynamic process of testing, learning, and the forging of a national identity.

The parallels between the Exodus narrative and other hero myths are subtle but significant. While other heroes faced physical challenges and internal struggles, Moses confronts a formidable political power and the daunting task of leading a large group through a difficult and potentially dangerous journey. His success depends not on his own physical prowess but on his unwavering faith, his ability to inspire faith in others, and the powerful intervention of a divine power. This unique blend of faith, leadership, and divine action distinguishes the Exodus story within the broader context of ancient hero myths. The narrative doesn't focus solely on the strength of the leader, but rather on the symbiotic relationship between the leader, the divine, and the people they are leading.

Furthermore, the Exodus story is not merely a historical account but also a foundational narrative for the Jewish people. It forms the basis of their national identity and continues to resonate with generations of Jews as a story of liberation, hope, and the enduring power of faith. The story's lasting influence transcends its historical context, speaking to universal themes of oppression, freedom, and the struggle for justice. It has inspired countless individuals and movements throughout history, serving as a powerful symbol of hope for the oppressed and a reminder of the importance of faith and perseverance in the face of adversity. The enduring appeal of the Exodus narrative lies in its ability to connect with audiences on both a historical and spiritual level, providing a timeless message of hope and liberation.

The comparison between Moses's leadership and the leadership of other figures discussed previously reveals fascinating insights. While Gilgamesh's leadership is often driven by personal ambition, and the Buddha's path is centered on self-discovery and inner peace, Moses's leadership is fundamentally about serving his people and enacting God's will. His heroism is not about personal glory or transcendence, but about collective liberation. This focus on the liberation of an entire group distinguishes him from the other figures discussed and positions the Exodus narrative as a compelling exploration of collective heroism and the power of faith in achieving societal transformation. The Exodus story transcends individual heroism, highlighting the collaborative effort necessary to overcome oppression and build a just and equitable society. The lasting impact of this narrative is not solely on the individual level, but also on the societal and spiritual realm, contributing to the development of a distinct religious identity and moral code.

In conclusion, the narrative of Moses and the Exodus offers a unique perspective on the archetype of the hero. It shifts the emphasis from individual strength and prowess to divine intervention, inspired leadership, and the collective struggle for liberation. The journey of the Israelites, from slavery to freedom, provides a powerful metaphor for the human longing for justice and the enduring power of faith in the face of adversity. The story's lasting impact lies in its universal themes of oppression, liberation, and the enduring human search for meaning and purpose within a larger divine context. The Exodus narrative, therefore, enriches the broader study of hero myths by highlighting a distinct form of heroism centered on faith, divine intervention, and the collective pursuit of freedom. The narrative resonates not just as a historical account, but as a powerful symbol of hope, resilience, and the enduring power of the human spirit in the face of seemingly insurmountable odds.

Shared Characteristics of Hero Myths Resilience and Transformation

The preceding chapters have explored a diverse array of hero myths, drawing from ancient Greek, Roman, Egyptian, Buddhist, and Abrahamic traditions. From Gilgamesh's quest for immortality to the Buddha's pursuit of enlightenment and Moses's liberation of the Israelites, these narratives, while vastly different in their specific details, reveal surprising commonalities. This section will synthesize these diverse narratives, highlighting the shared characteristics that contribute to their enduring power and influence across cultures and time.

One of the most striking shared characteristics is the concept of *resilience* . Each of these heroes, in their own way, faces seemingly insurmountable obstacles. Gilgamesh confronts the inevitability of death, a universal human fear, while Heracles battles monstrous creatures and performs seemingly impossible tasks. The Buddha grapples with the suffering inherent in existence, a struggle shared by all sentient beings. Even seemingly divinely favored heroes like Moses face immense challenges, navigating the perilous wilderness and confronting the power of the Pharaoh. Their resilience is not merely a matter of physical strength or exceptional skill. It stems from an inner fortitude, a capacity to endure hardship, overcome adversity, and persist in the face of setbacks. This internal resilience, often fueled by a strong sense of purpose or belief, is a defining trait of the heroic archetype. It is this ability to bounce back from failure, to learn from setbacks, and to continue striving towards a goal that renders these figures so inspiring. The perseverance displayed by these heroes reflects the human capacity to overcome seemingly insurmountable odds, a testament to the enduring strength of the human spirit.

Further reinforcing the concept of resilience is the repeated theme of *transformation* . The hero's journey is rarely a linear progression. Rather, it is a process of growth, change, and self-discovery. Gilgamesh, initially arrogant and self-centered, undergoes a profound transformation through his experiences, ultimately learning the value of friendship and accepting his mortality. Heracles, despite his superhuman strength, is not immune to human weakness; he learns from his mistakes, grows in wisdom, and achieves a measure of redemption. The Buddha's path to enlightenment is nothing less than a complete transformation of his perspective, moving from a life of luxury and privilege to a life of renunciation and spiritual pursuit. Moses too undergoes significant change, moving from a hesitant shepherd to a powerful leader capable of leading an entire nation towards freedom. This transformative aspect of the hero's journey speaks to the human potential for growth, change, and self-improvement. It demonstrates that even in the face of great adversity, individuals can evolve, learn, and ultimately become better versions of themselves.

The concept of *sacrifice* also emerges as a significant commonality. Each of these heroes, in their own way, makes sacrifices—sometimes willingly, sometimes unwillingly—in pursuit of their goals. Gilgamesh's quest for immortality necessitates significant sacrifices, both personal and physical. Heracles endures immense physical and mental strain in his labors. The Buddha renounces worldly possessions and comforts to pursue enlightenment. Moses, in his devotion to his people, faces threats to his own safety and well-being. These sacrifices, while varying in nature, underscore the theme of selflessness and dedication that is often associated with the heroic archetype. The willingness to sacrifice personal desires or comforts for a greater good speaks to the capacity for altruism within the human condition. These sacrifices aren't solely physical; they often entail the surrendering of personal ambition, comfort, and even safety. In these acts, we see the willingness to prioritize the well-being of others or a larger cause above one's own immediate needs.

Furthermore, the idea of a *helper or mentor* frequently appears. Gilgamesh is aided by Enkidu, his loyal companion. Heracles receives guidance from various gods and goddesses. The Buddha has various disciples who aid his work. Moses receives divine guidance and support throughout his journey. These figures provide assistance, guidance, and support, often acting as catalysts for the hero's growth and transformation. They offer crucial guidance, provide much-needed support, or even impart necessary skills and knowledge. The presence of these mentors underscores the importance of human connection and collaboration in achieving extraordinary feats. These supportive figures are not merely passive observers; they actively contribute to the hero's journey, offering advice, resources, and encouragement.

Finally, the concept of a *journey* is central to most hero myths. This is not necessarily a physical journey, although that aspect is frequently present. It is also an internal journey, a process of self-discovery, growth, and transformation. Gilgamesh's journey is both literal and metaphorical, taking him to the ends of the earth and into the depths of his own soul. The Buddha's journey is primarily an internal one, a process of self-reflection and spiritual awakening. Moses's journey is a combination of physical and spiritual elements, leading him and his people through the wilderness and toward a new beginning. These journeys, whether physical, spiritual, or psychological, emphasize the transformative power of experience. The challenges and trials encountered along the way serve as catalysts for growth, forcing the hero to confront their limitations and discover their true potential.

The enduring appeal of hero myths lies in their ability to reflect fundamental aspects of the human experience. They offer narratives that address universal themes such as mortality, suffering, the pursuit of meaning, the struggle for justice, and the capacity for both good and evil. They provide inspiration and hope, offering examples of resilience, perseverance, and transformation. These myths, while rooted in specific cultural contexts, tap into deeper human needs and aspirations. They offer models for behavior, ideals to strive toward, and cautionary tales to learn from. The shared characteristics discussed above – resilience, transformation, sacrifice, mentorship, and the journey itself – are not merely narrative devices. They resonate with audiences across cultures and time periods because they reflect fundamental aspects of the human condition. They provide us with a framework for understanding our own struggles, celebrating our triumphs, and finding inspiration in the face of adversity. The study of these ancient myths not only illuminates the beliefs and values of past societies but also provides valuable insights into the enduring human quest for meaning and purpose. Through the analysis of these parallel narratives, we are offered a glimpse into the timeless aspects of the human experience and the search for heroism within ourselves and our communities. The shared characteristics highlight the enduring human need for hope, inspiration, and a sense of purpose, needs that transcend cultural boundaries and the passage of time. These ancient stories continue to inspire and motivate us because they speak to the universal aspects of the human spirit, reminding us of our capacity for resilience, transformation, and the pursuit of a greater good.

The Ten Commandments and the JudeoChristian Ethical Framework

The exploration of ancient moral codes and ethical systems naturally leads us to a cornerstone of Judeo-Christian ethics: the Ten Commandments. Far from being a static, monolithic set of rules, the Decalogue, as it's known in Hebrew, possesses a rich history, evolving interpretation, and enduring influence on Western thought and law. Understanding its context is crucial to appreciating its impact. The commandments, traditionally attributed to Moses in the Book of Exodus, are not presented as an arbitrary list of prohibitions but rather as a framework for a covenant relationship between God and the Israelites. This covenant, a central concept in the Abrahamic faiths, involves reciprocal obligations: divine protection and guidance in exchange for obedience and adherence to a moral code.

The historical setting of the Ten Commandments is significant. The Israelites, having escaped slavery in Egypt, were forging a new national identity in a challenging environment. The commandments provided a framework for social cohesion, justice, and a distinct ethical framework separate from the surrounding cultures. They weren't presented in a vacuum; rather, they were designed to address specific social issues and challenges faced by a newly formed nation navigating a precarious existence in the ancient Near East. Comparing them to other ancient Near Eastern legal codes, like the Code of Hammurabi, reveals both similarities and striking differences. While Hammurabi’s code emphasized retribution and lex talionis ("an eye for an eye"), the Ten Commandments, while containing elements of justice, placed a greater emphasis on moral principles, personal responsibility, and a relationship with the divine. The focus shifted from merely punishing offenses to promoting a society grounded in ethical conduct.

The first three commandments address the relationship between humanity and God. The prohibition against other gods emphasizes monotheism, a radical concept in the polytheistic world of the ancient Near East. This insistence on a single, supreme God established a unique foundation for the Israelite identity and shaped their worldview. The prohibition against using God's name in vain underscores the importance of reverence and respect for the divine. The commandment regarding the Sabbath's observance not only established a day of rest but also provided a rhythm to life, a time for spiritual reflection and communal bonding, emphasizing the balance between work and spiritual life. These commandments, by setting the parameters of the relationship with God, establish the overarching moral framework for the remainder of the Decalogue.

The remaining seven commandments address interpersonal relationships and social behavior. The prohibitions against murder, adultery, and theft are universal ethical principles found in many cultures and legal systems. However, their inclusion within the divinely sanctioned framework of the Ten Commandments gave them immense weight and authority within the Israelite society. They formed the basis of their social contract, shaping not only individual behavior but also the fabric of their community. The commandment against bearing false witness underscored the importance of truthfulness, justice, and the integrity of testimony, crucial elements in any functioning legal system. The prohibition against coveting emphasizes the internal moral dimension, extending beyond outward actions to encompass intentions and desires. This internalization of morality is a significant aspect, distinguishing the commandments from purely externally imposed rules.

Interpreting the Ten Commandments has been a continuous process throughout history. Different religious and philosophical schools have approached the text from various angles, leading to varying understandings and applications. Some interpretations have focused on the literal meaning of each commandment, while others have emphasized the underlying principles and their implications for modern life. For example, the concept of “murder” has been debated extensively, with questions surrounding issues such as capital punishment, self-defense, and the morality of warfare. Similarly, the commandment against adultery has been interpreted in diverse ways, with differing perspectives on premarital sex, divorce, and same-sex relationships. The commandment regarding the Sabbath has also faced evolving interpretations over time, with discussions concerning its relevance in modern society and the concept of rest and spiritual renewal. These differing interpretations highlight the dynamic nature of ethical codes and their adaptation to changing social contexts.

The Ten Commandments' influence extends far beyond the Jewish faith. Christianity and Islam, both Abrahamic religions, have incorporated them, albeit with their own unique interpretations and expansions. The New Testament, while emphasizing love and grace, builds upon the ethical foundation laid by the Ten Commandments. Jesus' teachings, particularly the Sermon on the Mount, elaborate on the commandments, emphasizing the spirit of the law as much as its letter. Similarly, Islamic jurisprudence, based on the Quran and the Sunnah, incorporates core principles consistent with the Ten Commandments, emphasizing moral rectitude and social justice. The lasting influence of the Ten Commandments on Western legal systems is undeniable. Many legal codes, both secular and religious, reflect principles rooted in the commandments, particularly concerning issues such as murder, theft, and perjury. Concepts like justice, fairness, and personal responsibility, central to the commandments, have permeated Western legal thought and practice for centuries.

The study of the Ten Commandments leads to a broader discussion of the nature of law and ethics. Are moral laws divinely ordained, or are they the products of human reason and social agreement? This question has been the subject of intense debate throughout history, encompassing philosophical, theological, and legal discussions. Some argue that morality is inherently linked to a higher power, with the Ten Commandments representing a divine revelation of ethical principles. Others maintain that moral codes are social constructs, evolving to reflect changing societal values and needs. Regardless of one's perspective on this fundamental debate, the Ten Commandments undoubtedly represent a significant attempt to codify moral principles, shaping individual conduct and societal structures.

Beyond their legal and ethical implications, the Ten Commandments offer insights into the human condition. They reflect both our capacity for good and our potential for evil. They acknowledge human fallibility while simultaneously proposing a path toward moral betterment. The commandments serve as a constant reminder of the need for self-reflection, accountability, and the pursuit of a just and compassionate society. The enduring power of the Ten Commandments lies not solely in their age or their religious context, but in their ability to address fundamental questions of human existence, social interaction, and the pursuit of a moral life. They provide a framework for understanding our relationship with both God and our fellow humans, emphasizing the importance of respect, justice, and responsibility in all aspects of life. The continuing dialogue surrounding their interpretation underscores their ongoing relevance and their enduring impact on human thought and society. The challenge they pose, even in modern times, continues to stimulate reflection and debate on the nature of morality, justice, and the search for meaning in a complex world. The Ten Commandments, therefore, remain a potent symbol of the enduring quest for ethical conduct and societal harmony. The ongoing discussions and reinterpretations highlight their capacity to adapt to changing social norms while still retaining their core ethical principles, emphasizing their continuing relevance in a constantly evolving world.

The Principles of Maat in Ancient Egypt

The transition from the structured legalism of the Ten Commandments to the more nuanced concept of Ma'at in ancient Egypt provides a fascinating comparative study in ethical frameworks. While the Ten Commandments present a relatively explicit list of dos and don'ts, Ma'at represents a more holistic and deeply embedded moral order permeating all aspects of Egyptian life, from daily interactions to cosmic balance. It wasn't simply a set of rules, but rather a principle, a way of being, and a force that governed the universe and human society. Understanding Ma'at requires moving beyond a purely codified system towards a conceptual understanding of righteousness, truth, justice, and cosmic harmony.

Unlike the explicitly divine origin attributed to the Ten Commandments, the origins of Ma'at are intertwined with the very creation of the world. In Egyptian mythology, Ma'at is often personified as a goddess, frequently depicted as a feather, symbolizing truth and balance. She is inextricably linked to the creator god, Ra, and is considered a fundamental aspect of his divine order. The act of creation itself was an act of establishing Ma'at, bringing order from chaos. This cosmic dimension of Ma'at distinguishes it from many other ancient ethical systems, which primarily focus on human interactions and social structures. For the Egyptians, maintaining Ma'at was not just a moral imperative, but a crucial element in the ongoing cosmic balance.

The concept of Ma'at extended far beyond a simple code of conduct. It permeated every aspect of Egyptian life, influencing their religious beliefs, political structures, social interactions, and even their daily routines. Maintaining Ma'at was seen as a sacred duty, essential not only for individual well-being but also for the stability of the entire universe. Violation of Ma'at was believed to disrupt the cosmic order, bringing about chaos and disorder. This belief system profoundly impacted the Egyptian worldview, influencing their perception of themselves, their society, and the cosmos.

The Pharaoh, as the earthly representative of Ra, played a pivotal role in upholding Ma'at. He was considered the supreme mediator between the divine and the human realms. His responsibility was not only to rule justly and efficiently but to actively maintain the cosmic balance by ensuring the proper performance of rituals, the preservation of temples, and the fair administration of justice. The Pharaoh's legitimacy and authority were directly tied to his ability to maintain Ma'at. Any deviation from this ideal could threaten his rule and lead to instability within the kingdom. This close link between leadership and cosmic order significantly differed from the more secular approaches to governance found in other ancient civilizations.

The concept of justice within Ma'at was not merely punitive but restorative. The goal was not simply to punish offenders but to restore balance and harmony. The "Weighing of the Heart" ceremony, prominently featured in the Book of the Dead, perfectly illustrates this concept. Upon death, the deceased's heart was weighed against the feather of Ma'at. If the heart was lighter than the feather, symbolizing a life lived in accordance with Ma'at, the individual was granted entry into the afterlife. However, if the heart was heavier, signifying a life of injustice and wrongdoing, it was devoured by the monstrous devourer Ammit, resulting in annihilation. This powerful metaphor highlighted the importance of striving for a life aligned with Ma'at, emphasizing the consequences of actions beyond mere earthly repercussions.

The practical application of Ma'at in daily life was multifaceted. Honest dealings, fairness in trade, respect for elders, and the equitable distribution of resources were all considered vital aspects of upholding Ma'at. These principles were ingrained in the social fabric of Egyptian society, shaping interactions between individuals, families, and communities. The emphasis on social harmony and mutual respect reflected a deeply ingrained societal value system, promoting cooperation and stability. This emphasis on social cohesion through ethical conduct contrasts with systems that primarily relied on laws and punishments to maintain order.

Art, literature, and architecture also served as important vehicles for reinforcing the concept of Ma'at. Numerous depictions of Ma'at appear in Egyptian art, often portraying her as a graceful and serene goddess, representing the ideal of balance and harmony. Pharaonic inscriptions frequently invoked Ma'at, emphasizing the ruler's commitment to upholding this essential principle. The grandeur of Egyptian temples and monuments, constructed with meticulous care and precision, reflected the Egyptians' dedication to creating a physical manifestation of Ma'at, a tangible expression of order and beauty in their world.

The enduring legacy of Ma'at is remarkable. Its influence can be traced through various aspects of Egyptian culture and religion for millennia. While the specific religious beliefs and practices of ancient Egypt evolved over time, the core principle of Ma'at remained a constant, a guiding force that shaped Egyptian society and culture. Its enduring appeal lies in its holistic nature, emphasizing a harmonious relationship between humans and the cosmos, and a moral framework emphasizing justice, truth, and balance.

Comparing Ma'at with the Ten Commandments reveals significant differences in approach. The Ten Commandments present a relatively rigid set of rules with clearly defined prohibitions. Ma'at, on the other hand, is a more fluid and nuanced concept, emphasizing a way of being rather than simply adherence to a specific set of laws. The Ten Commandments primarily focus on the relationship between humanity and God, and interpersonal interactions, while Ma'at encompasses a broader cosmic dimension, linking individual actions to the overall cosmic balance. Yet, both systems share the common goal of establishing a moral framework for society, promoting justice, and encouraging ethical behavior. The different approaches, however, reflect the unique cultural and religious contexts of their respective civilizations.

The significance of Ma'at extends beyond a simple comparison with other ancient ethical systems. Its holistic nature, emphasizing cosmic order, individual responsibility, and social harmony, continues to resonate even today. The principles of truth, justice, and balance remain universally valued, making the study of Ma'at relevant not only to historians and religious scholars but also to anyone seeking to understand the enduring human quest for meaning and moral purpose. The emphasis on living in harmony with the universe and one's fellow humans offers a timeless perspective on ethical conduct and the pursuit of a just and peaceful society. In a world often characterized by conflict and imbalance, the Egyptian concept of Ma'at offers a powerful and enduring message of hope, suggesting a path towards a more harmonious and equitable future. The pursuit of Ma'at, in its essence, is a constant striving for balance, a continuous effort to align individual actions with cosmic order, and a commitment to creating a world where justice and truth prevail. This striving remains a relevant and inspirational ideal in the modern world, reminding us of the profound connections between our individual actions and the well-being of the larger cosmos.

Buddhist Ethics and the Eightfold Path

The transition from the explicitly codified morality of the Ten Commandments and the holistic cosmic order of Ma'at brings us to a consideration of Buddhist ethics, a system profoundly different yet sharing common ground with its predecessors in its pursuit of a moral life. Buddhist ethics, unlike the primarily divinely ordained systems previously discussed, focuses on individual self-cultivation and the cessation of suffering through the practice of the Eightfold Path. This path, far from being a simple set of rules, is a multifaceted approach to ethical living, interwoven with practices of mindfulness, meditation, and the development of wisdom. While the Ten Commandments offer a relatively rigid framework of prohibitions, and Ma'at emphasizes a harmonious relationship with the cosmic order, the Eightfold Path offers a more nuanced and practical approach to ethical conduct.

Central to the Eightfold Path is the concept of *right conduct* , which encompasses three key aspects: right speech, right action, and right livelihood. Right speech emphasizes truthful communication, avoiding gossip, harsh language, and idle chatter. The emphasis is not simply on avoiding falsehood, but on cultivating a compassionate and constructive form of communication that promotes harmony and understanding. This resonates with the Egyptian emphasis on Ma'at's principle of truth, but it moves beyond a simple adherence to factual accuracy to a mindful consideration of the impact of words on others. Unlike the potentially punitive implications of violating the Ten Commandments, the focus in Buddhism is on cultivating skillful communication as a means of reducing suffering and fostering positive relationships. This is a practical application of ethical principles, emphasizing the impact of individual actions on the social and emotional well-being of the community.

Right action, the second element of right conduct, delves deeper into the realm of ethical behavior. It encompasses abstaining from actions that cause harm, whether physical, mental, or emotional. This includes refraining from killing, stealing, and sexual misconduct, actions that are also condemned in other ethical systems. However, the Buddhist understanding extends beyond simple adherence to rules. It involves cultivating a sense of compassion and non-violence that permeates all aspects of one's actions. This isn't merely about avoiding specific acts; it's about cultivating a mindset that prioritizes the well-being of all beings. This aligns with the restorative justice inherent in the concept of Ma'at, aiming not just to punish wrongdoing but to prevent future harm through mindful action. While the Ten Commandments provide a list of prohibited acts, the Buddhist approach emphasizes the cultivation of a virtuous character that naturally leads to ethical behavior.

Right livelihood, the third aspect of right conduct, emphasizes the importance of earning a living in a way that aligns with ethical principles. This means avoiding professions that cause harm or exploit others. For instance, occupations involving violence, deception, or the exploitation of resources would be considered unethical. Buddhist texts often encourage professions that promote well-being, such as farming, medicine, or teaching. This highlights the interconnectedness of ethical conduct and one's role in society, suggesting that a virtuous life encompasses all aspects of one's existence, not just personal interactions. This principle contrasts with the more limited scope of ethical guidelines found in some other systems, extending ethical considerations to the realm of economic activity and professional choices. The emphasis is on minimizing harm and maximizing benefit, aligning individual actions with the larger goals of reducing suffering and promoting collective well-being.

Beyond right conduct, the Eightfold Path emphasizes the development of *right mindfulness* , which involves cultivating a heightened awareness of one's thoughts, feelings, and actions. This is achieved through various meditative practices, allowing individuals to observe their internal states without judgment. This mindful awareness is crucial for ethical conduct, as it allows individuals to recognize the potential consequences of their actions before acting. It's a proactive approach to ethical living, preventing harm by fostering self-awareness and careful consideration of one's behavior. This differs from systems relying primarily on external rules and regulations. The internal focus on mindful awareness empowers individuals to make conscious ethical choices, rather than simply reacting to external pressures or social expectations. The cultivation of mindfulness is a key component in the development of ethical conduct within the Buddhist framework, acting as a preventative measure rather than a reactive one.

The cultivation of wisdom, the final aspect of the Eightfold Path, further enhances ethical conduct. Right understanding and right thought are crucial components in developing a clear understanding of the nature of reality and the causes of suffering. This wisdom guides ethical behavior, providing a framework for making sound moral judgments. It is through the development of wisdom that individuals can transcend the limitations of ego-centric thinking and develop a sense of compassion and empathy that motivates ethical action. Unlike systems relying solely on codified rules, the Buddhist approach encourages a deeper understanding of the root causes of suffering, leading to more effective and compassionate responses to ethical dilemmas. This deeper understanding shapes the individual's moral framework, providing a basis for ethical decision-making that is informed by wisdom and compassion, rather than merely adherence to rules.

The interplay between these elements of the Eightfold Path highlights the holistic nature of Buddhist ethics. It's not simply a matter of following a set of rules; it's a comprehensive approach to cultivating a virtuous life through right conduct, mindfulness, and wisdom. This integrated approach contrasts with the more compartmentalized ethical systems discussed earlier. The Buddhist framework emphasizes the interdependence of actions, thoughts, and intentions, suggesting that ethical living is not merely about external behavior but also a profound inner transformation. This emphasis on inner transformation is a key feature that sets it apart from other ancient ethical systems, highlighting the importance of self-cultivation and personal responsibility in the pursuit of ethical living.

Furthermore, the Buddhist concept of karma further reinforces the importance of ethical conduct. The principle of karma suggests that actions have consequences, not necessarily in a divinely ordained system of reward and punishment, but rather in the natural unfolding of cause and effect. Ethical actions lead to positive consequences, both for the individual and for others, while unethical actions lead to negative consequences. This emphasis on cause and effect provides a natural impetus for ethical behavior, independent of external sanctions or divine judgment. The individual is empowered to shape their own destiny through mindful actions, understanding that ethical conduct leads to positive outcomes, while unethical actions create negative consequences in the long term. This understanding reinforces the self-regulatory aspects of the Eightfold Path.

The Eightfold Path's emphasis on individual self-cultivation distinguishes it from systems that rely heavily on external authority or divine mandates. The responsibility for ethical conduct rests squarely on the individual, who is empowered through practice and self-awareness to cultivate a virtuous life. This self-empowerment reflects a profound shift in ethical thinking, moving away from external control towards personal responsibility and inner transformation. While external factors may influence behavior, the ultimate responsibility for ethical conduct rests with the individual, a key distinction from the divinely mandated ethical systems discussed earlier.

In conclusion, Buddhist ethics, as embodied in the Eightfold Path, presents a nuanced and holistic approach to ethical living. While sharing common ground with other ancient ethical systems in the pursuit of a moral life, its emphasis on individual self-cultivation, mindful awareness, and the development of wisdom distinguishes it profoundly. The focus on right conduct, right mindfulness, and the cultivation of wisdom offers a practical and comprehensive path to ethical living, emphasizing personal responsibility and the transformative power of self-awareness. The interconnectedness of these elements underscores the holistic nature of the Buddhist ethical framework, demonstrating a path to ethical conduct that is both rigorous and deeply personal. The enduring relevance of the Eightfold Path lies in its emphasis on inner transformation as the foundation for ethical living, a timeless message applicable to individuals and societies seeking a path to peace, harmony, and well-being.

Greek and Roman Stoicism and its Ethical Principles

The transition from the profoundly introspective ethical framework of Buddhism brings us to the seemingly contrasting, yet surprisingly complementary, philosophy of Stoicism. Flourishing in ancient Greece and Rome, Stoicism, unlike Buddhism's emphasis on inner transformation through meditation and mindfulness, presented a pragmatic and socially engaged approach to ethical living. While superficially different in their methods, both share a core commitment to reducing suffering and cultivating inner peace, albeit through different pathways.

Stoicism, founded by Zeno of Citium in the 3rd century BC, emphasized virtue as the sole good and the only path to *eudaimonia* , often translated as flourishing or living well. This wasn't a passive acceptance of fate, but an active pursuit of virtue through reason and self-control. Unlike systems focusing on external rewards or punishments, Stoicism placed the locus of ethical action firmly within the individual's capacity for rational thought and moral judgment. The Stoic sage, the ideal individual, was characterized by their unwavering commitment to virtue, regardless of external circumstances.

Central to Stoic ethics is the concept of *virtue* . Stoics identified four cardinal virtues: wisdom, justice, courage, and temperance. Wisdom encompasses practical wisdom, the ability to make sound judgments and live a life guided by reason. It's not merely intellectual knowledge, but the ability to apply knowledge to navigate life's complexities and make ethical choices. Justice, for Stoics, involved acting fairly and equitably towards others, recognizing the interconnectedness of human beings and upholding social harmony. This wasn't simply a matter of obeying laws, but of internalizing principles of fairness and acting justly even when it's personally difficult or disadvantageous. Courage, in the Stoic context, wasn't merely the absence of fear, but the ability to face adversity and act rightly despite fear or hardship. This involved understanding that external events are largely beyond one's control, and focusing instead on one's internal response and commitment to virtuous action. Finally, temperance involved self-control and moderation in all things, resisting excessive desires and impulses that could lead to suffering or harm. This wasn't asceticism, but a mindful approach to pleasure and avoidance of excess.

The Stoic emphasis on reason is inextricably linked to their understanding of virtue. Reason, for Stoics, was the faculty that allowed individuals to understand the natural order of the universe and their place within it. By understanding this natural order, individuals could align their actions with reason and virtue, thereby achieving *eudaimonia* . This involved accepting what is beyond one's control – external events, the actions of others, even one's own body – while focusing energy on what is within one's control: one's thoughts, judgments, and actions. This distinction between what is within and beyond our control is a cornerstone of Stoic philosophy and its ethical framework. By accepting the inevitable and focusing on the controllable, individuals could minimize suffering and cultivate inner peace, even amidst adversity.

Stoicism offered a practical framework for navigating everyday life, providing tools and techniques for managing emotions and responding to challenging situations. This practicality set it apart from some other philosophical schools of the time that focused primarily on abstract speculation. Stoic practices, such as negative visualization –

contemplating potential misfortunes to lessen their impact when they occur – and journaling – reflecting on one's thoughts and actions to improve self-awareness – are still relevant today. These techniques aimed at cultivating inner resilience and emotional regulation, allowing individuals to maintain composure and act virtuously even under pressure. The emphasis on self-reliance and self-mastery within Stoicism also resonated with many, offering a sense of agency and empowerment in a world that often felt chaotic and unpredictable.

The Stoic emphasis on living in accordance with nature extended beyond personal conduct to encompass social responsibility. Stoics believed in the interconnectedness of all beings and emphasized the importance of living harmoniously within society. This involved fulfilling one's social roles and duties, contributing to the common good, and treating others with respect and compassion. While individual virtue was central, Stoics didn't advocate for withdrawal from society. Instead, they saw active participation in social life as a crucial aspect of living a virtuous life. This social dimension of Stoicism is often overlooked, but it's a vital aspect of their ethical framework. Their commitment to social harmony and justice reflects a sophisticated understanding of the intricate relationship between individual well-being and the collective good.

The Stoic understanding of happiness or flourishing, *eudaimonia* , differed significantly from hedonistic approaches. It wasn't about maximizing pleasure or minimizing pain, but about living a virtuous life in accordance with reason. External factors like wealth, health, or reputation were considered "indifferents," neither good nor bad in themselves. While not to be rejected, they were not the source of true happiness. True happiness, for the Stoic, derived from inner peace, which is achieved through virtuous action and acceptance of what is beyond one's control. This focus on internal states, rather than external circumstances, reflects a resilient and adaptable ethical framework that transcended the vicissitudes of fate.

Roman Stoicism, building upon its Greek foundations, found fertile ground in the Roman Empire. Figures like Seneca, Epictetus, and Marcus Aurelius adapted and expanded Stoic philosophy, shaping its influence on Roman society and leaving behind enduring literary works that continue to be studied and appreciated. Seneca's letters and essays offer practical advice on living a virtuous life, while Epictetus's *Enchiridion* provides concise summaries of core Stoic principles. Marcus Aurelius's *Meditations* , a personal journal of reflections, offers profound insights into the challenges of leadership and the pursuit of inner peace amidst the pressures of imperial power. These texts showcase the adaptability and enduring relevance of Stoicism, its capacity to resonate with individuals across diverse contexts and circumstances.

Despite its emphasis on reason and self-control, Stoicism wasn't a cold or emotionless philosophy. Stoics recognized the importance of emotions, but they emphasized the need to manage and regulate them, avoiding excessive emotional reactions that could lead to suffering. This wasn't about suppressing emotions, but about understanding their origins and responding to them rationally. The aim was to cultivate a balanced emotional state, neither excessively joyful nor excessively sorrowful, but rather a state of inner tranquility and resilience. This emotional regulation was not merely a personal benefit; it also served as a foundation for ethical action, preventing emotional impulses from undermining rational judgment and virtuous behavior. The Stoic ideal wasn't emotional detachment, but emotional wisdom.

In contrast to the divinely ordained ethical systems explored earlier, Stoicism presented a secular framework for ethical living. While not rejecting the existence of gods, it didn't base its ethics on divine commands or supernatural rewards and punishments. Instead, its ethical principles were grounded in reason and the understanding of the natural order. This secular foundation gave Stoicism a unique appeal in a world increasingly characterized by diverse religious beliefs and practices. Its emphasis on reason and individual responsibility provided a framework for ethical conduct that transcended religious differences, emphasizing shared human values and the pursuit of a virtuous life. This broad applicability continues to resonate with those seeking ethical guidance independent of specific religious doctrines.

The enduring legacy of Greek and Roman Stoicism lies in its emphasis on virtue, reason, and self-control as the foundation for ethical living. While differing from other ancient ethical systems in its methods and emphasis, it shares a common goal: the pursuit of a fulfilling and virtuous life. Its practical tools for managing emotions and navigating life's challenges, its focus on personal responsibility, and its secular foundation continue to inspire individuals seeking meaning and purpose in the modern world. The enduring relevance of Stoicism demonstrates the timeless human desire for a life guided by reason, virtue, and inner peace. Its adaptability and enduring appeal testify to the universality of its core principles and its capacity to offer practical guidance for ethical living across cultures and eras. The exploration of Stoicism highlights the diverse approaches humanity has taken in the quest for moral clarity and a life well-lived, demonstrating the ongoing relevance of ancient wisdom in shaping contemporary ethical thought.

Comparative Analysis of Ethical Systems Universal Moral Principles

The preceding chapters have journeyed through a diverse tapestry of ancient ethical systems, from the introspective path of Buddhism to the pragmatic approach of Stoicism, each offering a unique perspective on the good life and the pursuit of virtue. Now, it is time to step back and examine the common threads that bind these seemingly disparate systems, exploring the surprising convergence of moral principles across vastly different cultures and time periods. While the specific practices and rituals may differ dramatically, a closer examination reveals a remarkable degree of shared understanding regarding fundamental human values.

One of the most striking parallels lies in the emphasis on self-control and the cultivation of inner peace. Whether it is the Buddhist practice of mindfulness, the Stoic emphasis on reason and self-mastery, or the Confucian focus on self-cultivation, a recurring theme emerges: the importance of managing one's thoughts, emotions, and actions to achieve inner harmony. This is not merely a matter of personal well-being; it also forms the foundation for ethical conduct. An individual who lacks self-control is far less likely to act justly or compassionately, to resist temptation or overcome adversity. The control of the self, then, is not simply a personal virtue, but a crucial prerequisite for ethical action within the broader community.

Furthermore, the concept of compassion and empathy features prominently across these diverse ethical systems. Buddhist teachings emphasize compassion (karuna) as a cornerstone of the path to enlightenment, highlighting the interconnectedness of all beings and the importance of alleviating suffering. Confucianism stresses *ren* , often translated as benevolence or humaneness, encompassing compassion, empathy, and a deep concern for others. While not always explicitly articulated in the same manner, a similar emphasis on concern for others, on treating others with respect and dignity, can be found in Stoicism's emphasis on justice and social harmony, and even within the broader framework of ancient Egyptian ethical precepts which prioritized Ma'at (truth, justice, and cosmic order) as the foundation of a just society. This shared emphasis on compassion and empathy underscores the deeply human need for connection and the recognition of the inherent dignity of all individuals.

Another consistent principle across these varied ethical frameworks is the importance of justice. The pursuit of justice, however, is understood in nuanced ways depending on the system under consideration. In the context of ancient Near Eastern traditions, justice is frequently connected with divine law and retribution. The concept of Ma'at in ancient Egypt, for example, not only emphasizes justice within human society but also links it to the cosmic order, suggesting a divine sanction for ethical conduct. This echoes the Abrahamic traditions, where divine commandments serve as a moral compass, with punishments or rewards seen as consequences of ethical or unethical behaviour. Stoicism, however, articulates justice from a more secular perspective, emphasizing fairness, equity, and rational action in accordance with natural law, rather than relying on a divine mandate. Confucianism, though infused with a deep respect for tradition and ancestral wisdom, similarly emphasizes the importance of acting justly within society, upholding social harmony and order through ethical conduct.

The pursuit of wisdom also appears as a unifying theme across many of these systems. Whether it is Buddhist prajna (wisdom) leading to understanding of emptiness, Stoic sophrosyne (self-knowledge and moderation) aiding rational decision-making, or Confucian junzi (the ideal moral person), embodying wisdom and virtue, the quest for wisdom consistently emerges as a crucial element in achieving ethical excellence. This wisdom isn't simply intellectual knowledge, but a practical understanding of human nature, the social fabric, and one's place within a larger cosmos. It entails both theoretical understanding and the capacity for virtuous action in everyday life, effectively bridging the gap between philosophical insight and practical conduct.

The concept of virtue, though expressed through diverse terminology and conceptions, forms another significant commonality. The ancient Greeks, for example, identified various virtues, emphasizing courage, justice, wisdom, and temperance, a similar framework underpinning the Stoic ethical system. Buddhism does not employ the term "virtue" in the same way, yet qualities like compassion, mindfulness, and generosity directly correspond to the core virtues highlighted by Greek philosophy. Similarly, Confucianism emphasizes virtues such as benevolence, righteousness, propriety, wisdom, and trustworthiness, reflecting a parallel ethical framework focused on character development and virtuous conduct. While the precise definition of virtues might vary, the overarching principle remains consistent: the pursuit of ethical excellence through character development.

However, important distinctions exist within the methods and the means by which ethical goals are pursued. The approach of Buddhism, for instance, hinges significantly on individual self-cultivation through practices such as meditation, mindfulness, and ethical conduct. The emphasis is on internal transformation leading to liberation from suffering. Conversely, Stoicism, although emphasising self-cultivation, presents a more overtly pragmatic and socially engaged path to virtue. Confucianism underscores the importance of social harmony and filial piety, with ethical conduct viewed primarily through the lens of one's social roles and responsibilities. These variations highlight the different cultural and societal contexts that shape the articulation and application of overarching ethical principles. These differences, however, do not necessarily negate the underlying shared emphasis on virtue, inner harmony, and compassionate action.

Despite their diverse contexts and historical periods, these ancient ethical systems offer valuable insights for contemporary ethical thought. The enduring emphasis on self-control, compassion, justice, wisdom, and virtue provides a framework for navigating the complexities of the modern world. The emphasis on the interconnectedness of individuals, the importance of social harmony, and the need for ethical action in everyday life offer guidance for shaping a more just and compassionate society. The insights of ancient thinkers, although expressed through different languages and methodologies, continue to resonate deeply with contemporary moral considerations and provide a rich source of guidance for ethical deliberation.

In conclusion, while surface differences exist between various ancient ethical systems, a remarkable convergence emerges when one examines the underlying moral principles. The emphasis on self-control, compassion, justice, wisdom, and virtue points towards a fundamental human desire for ethical living, for a life lived in harmony with oneself, with others, and with the natural world. The variations in the expression and implementation of these principles reflect diverse cultural contexts and historical circumstances, yet the core values remain consistent, underscoring the timeless and universal appeal of ethical living. The shared principles across these different systems highlight the inherent human capacity for moral reasoning and the enduring quest for meaning and purpose within a complex and challenging world. The study of these ancient ethical systems, therefore, provides not only historical insight but also a profound and continuing source of moral guidance for the modern age. The enduring relevance of these ancient wisdom traditions underscores the fundamental human need for ethical frameworks that guide conduct, provide meaning, and promote a life well-lived.

The Olympian Gods of Ancient Greece and Rome

The preceding discussion highlighted the surprising convergence of ethical principles across diverse ancient traditions. However, the expression of these principles often took the form of narratives, myths, and religious systems, which varied significantly in their specifics. To further illuminate the cross-cultural parallels in understanding morality and the human condition, we now turn our attention to the Olympian pantheon of ancient Greece and Rome, examining how their myths and the roles of their deities reflected and shaped societal values. While significantly different in their specific rituals and practices, the shared narratives within these pantheons reveal common anxieties and aspirations reflecting fundamental aspects of the human experience.

The Olympian gods of ancient Greece, with their complex relationships, triumphs, and flaws, offered a model of both ideal behavior and the dangers of unchecked power. Zeus, the king of the gods, epitomized authority but was also known for his infidelity and capricious nature, a reflection of the complexities of leadership and the potential for abuse of power. His very existence and actions served as a cautionary tale, albeit one embedded within a complex system of belief and ritual. His numerous affairs and illegitimate children, often portrayed in both comical and tragic narratives, highlighted the consequences of unchecked desire and the disruption this could cause within the divine realm and the human world. These narratives functioned as a societal commentary on the dangers of tyranny and the importance of justice, even among the immortals.

Hera, Zeus's wife and sister, embodied the concept of marriage and family, albeit in a particularly turbulent and challenging example. Her jealousy and vindictiveness towards Zeus's lovers and their offspring, while often portrayed comedically, underscored the importance of marital fidelity and the societal consequences of its violation. Her struggles reflected the complexities of female power within a patriarchal structure, highlighting both the strength and the limitations faced by women in their attempts to maintain authority and control. Her role also served as a cautionary tale about the destructive nature of unchecked envy and the importance of self-control even in the face of provocation.

Poseidon, god of the sea, represented the unpredictable and often destructive forces of nature. His temperamental nature and ability to unleash storms and earthquakes served as a constant reminder of humanity's vulnerability and dependence on the whims of a powerful and often unforgiving natural world. His myths highlight the importance of respecting nature's power and the consequences of ignoring or challenging its overwhelming might. His role as a god who is both feared and respected served as a powerful societal symbol of the need for caution and reverence in the face of nature's forces.

Athena, goddess of wisdom, strategy, and warfare, represented intellectual prowess and the rational pursuit of goals. Her association with Athens itself served as a powerful symbol of the city's strategic thinking and its emphasis on intellectual and artistic achievement. Unlike many of her fellow Olympians, Athena consistently demonstrated qualities of self-control, strategic thinking, and a commitment to justice, offering an idealized example of both intellectual and moral virtue. She offered a counterpoint to the often impulsive and emotional actions of the other gods, showcasing the benefits of rationality, planning, and forethought.

Apollo, god of light, music, and prophecy, embodied artistic and intellectual pursuits, but also represented the complexities of human rationality and the danger of pride. His association with prophecy highlighted the ambiguous nature of knowledge and the potential for both insight and delusion. His many romances and their often tragic consequences also underscored the potential for self-destruction when guided by intense emotions, thus tempering the glorification of intellect and artistic pursuits with a dose of caution. His complex and multifaceted personality demonstrated the human capacity for both brilliance and fallibility.

Ares, god of war, epitomized unbridled aggression and violence. Unlike Athena's strategic approach to warfare, Ares represented the raw, untamed energy of conflict and the destructive consequences of unchecked rage. He served as a stark reminder of the potential for violence inherent in human nature, and the devastation it can unleash. His unpopularity among both gods and mortals highlights the societal understanding of the destructive potential of uncontrolled aggression and the need for a more tempered and strategic approach to conflict.

Aphrodite, goddess of love and beauty, represented the powerful and often unpredictable forces of desire and passion. Her involvement in numerous intricate and often tragic love affairs highlighted the potentially destructive nature of unchecked passion and the complexities of romantic relationships. Her influence on both gods and mortals underscored the pervasive nature of human desire and its influence on decisions and actions. Her role within the pantheon served as a cautionary tale on the dangers of obsession and the potential for love to cause both joy and devastation.

Hephaestus, the god of fire and metalworking, provided a counterpoint to the more dramatic and emotionally driven Olympian deities. His skill and craftsmanship demonstrated the importance of diligence, skill, and dedication to one's craft, highlighting the value of practical skills and the contribution of artisans to society. His role as a creator of both tools and weapons also demonstrated the duality of human ingenuity, capable of both creative construction and destructive power. His somewhat marginalized position within the Olympian family, despite his vital contributions, also hints at broader societal understandings of the roles and status of different social groups.

Hermes, the messenger god, embodied communication, trade, and travel, embodying the human desire for connection and exchange. His cleverness and cunning underscored the importance of resourcefulness and adaptability, and his role as a go-between highlighted the complexities of communication and the potential for both positive and negative effects. His position bridging the divine and mortal worlds underscored the complex relationship between humanity and the divine, a relationship characterized by both interaction and the acknowledgment of a transcendent power.

These Olympian deities, with their varied attributes and complex relationships, reflected and shaped the values and anxieties of ancient Greek society. Their stories provided moral lessons, explored the complexities of human nature, and offered a framework for understanding the world around them, including the inherent uncertainties and the necessity of navigating the power dynamics both within human society and the larger cosmos. The narrative structure of these myths served as a powerful pedagogical tool, conveying social lessons, moral codes, and expectations in a compelling and memorable way.

The Roman adoption of the Greek pantheon demonstrated both continuity and adaptation. While the Roman gods largely retained their Greek counterparts' attributes and narratives, Roman interpretations often emphasized different aspects, reflecting Roman societal values and political structures. The emphasis on civic duty, military prowess, and the stability of the state played a significant role in how Roman culture interpreted and integrated these deities into its own belief system.

Jupiter, the Roman equivalent of Zeus, retained the role of king of the gods, but his association with Roman imperial authority and the concept of *pietas* (duty to family, state, and gods) highlighted the importance of obedience and loyalty to the established order. Juno, the Roman counterpart of Hera, took on a similar role but her association with Roman marital ideals and the state's welfare emphasized the importance of upholding traditional family structures and ensuring the stability of the Roman state. Mars, the god of war, gained prominence as the patron god of Rome, reflecting the city's emphasis on military strength and expansion. His role shifted to reflect Rome's military ethos and ambition, unlike the more chaotic portrayal of Ares in Greek mythology.

The Roman pantheon demonstrated a clear adaptation to the values and political structure of the Roman Empire. The gods retained their core attributes, but their emphasis shifted to reflect the Roman emphasis on order, stability, and civic duty. The narratives surrounding the gods continued to offer moral instruction and a framework for understanding the human condition, but the interpretations and emphasis reflected Roman societal priorities and political structures. This highlights how religious narratives are not static but are constantly reinterpreted and adapted to the changing context of cultures and societies. The remarkable longevity of the Olympian tradition, with its consistent themes and adaptability across cultures, points to a fundamental human need to create meaningful narratives that explore the human condition and the complex relationship between humanity and the cosmos. The lasting influence of these myths, both in the ancient world and in subsequent literary and artistic traditions, underscores their profound and continuing relevance. Their enduring appeal testifies to the power of mythology to shape moral frameworks, express social anxieties, and inspire creative expression. The parallels between the Greek and Roman pantheons demonstrate the commonalities of religious thought and the ability of narratives to transcend cultural boundaries, offering a glimpse into universal themes, fears, and aspirations. The consistent themes across these traditions, despite the differences in details, point toward shared fundamental aspects of the human condition and the enduring search for meaning and purpose.

The Egyptian Pantheon and its Hierarchy

The Egyptian pantheon, unlike the neatly structured Olympian system, presented a more fluid and multifaceted hierarchy, reflecting the complexities of ancient Egyptian society and its evolving beliefs over millennia. While not as rigidly defined as the Olympian hierarchy, the Egyptian pantheon possessed a central core of powerful deities, with numerous lesser gods and goddesses orbiting around them, often associated with specific localities, aspects of nature, or human activities. The relationships between these deities were dynamic, sometimes cooperative, sometimes competitive, and often reflecting the changing political landscapes and social structures of ancient Egypt.

At the apex of the pantheon stood the creator god, often identified as Atum, Ra, or a combination of both, representing the sun god and the force that brought the world into existence. Atum, often depicted as a self-created deity emerging from the primordial waters of Nun, symbolized the generative power of creation itself. His association with the setting sun reflected the cyclical nature of life and death, a prominent theme in ancient Egyptian religious thought. Ra, the sun god, was often portrayed as sailing across the sky in his solar barque, bringing life and light to the world. His daily journey across the heavens and his nightly descent into the underworld symbolized the cycle of regeneration and renewal. The fusion of Atum and Ra into Atum-Ra emphasized the combination of creative and life-giving power, highlighting the interconnectedness of creation and the sun's vital role in sustaining life. The pharaohs frequently identified themselves as the earthly representatives of Ra, reinforcing the divine legitimacy of their rule.

Osiris, god of the underworld and vegetation, held a pivotal position within the Egyptian pantheon, representing death, resurrection, and the cyclical nature of life. His myth, a narrative of murder, dismemberment, and resurrection, served as a powerful metaphor for the cyclical processes of nature and the promise of rebirth. Osiris's death and resurrection ensured the fertile flooding of the Nile, providing life-sustaining waters for agriculture, and becoming a powerful symbol of hope and renewal. His wife and sister, Isis, played a crucial role in this narrative, demonstrating remarkable resourcefulness and devotion in piecing Osiris's body back together and conceiving Horus, their son, through magical means. Isis became a powerful goddess associated with magic, motherhood, and healing, symbolizing feminine power and resilience.

Horus, the son of Isis and Osiris, inherited his father's role as king of the gods after avenging his father's murder by setting against his uncle Set. Horus represented kingship, strength, and the power of the pharaohs, often depicted as a falcon or a man with a falcon's head. Horus's victory over Set represented the triumph of order over chaos and the cyclical renewal of kingship. The narrative of Horus’s conflict with Set showcased the Egyptians’ understanding of the struggle between order and chaos, highlighting the importance of maintaining cosmic balance.

Set, god of chaos, storms, and the desert, represented the disruptive forces of nature and the challenges to order. While often portrayed as a villainous figure, Set was not simply a force of pure evil. He played a crucial role in maintaining cosmic balance, representing the unpredictable and sometimes destructive aspects of the natural world. His defeat by Horus highlighted the importance of overcoming chaos and maintaining order, but also acknowledged the ever-present potential for disorder and disruption.

Other major deities enriched the complexities of the Egyptian pantheon. Geb, god of the earth, and Nut, goddess of the sky, embodied the primal elements of creation and represented the fundamental relationship between the earth and the heavens. Their children, Osiris, Isis, Set, and Nephthys, played pivotal roles in the unfolding of cosmic dramas, emphasizing the interconnectedness of the various deities and the importance of maintaining balance in the cosmos. Thoth, god of writing, wisdom, and magic, occupied a unique position as a mediator and guide, associated with both divine and human realms. He often served as a counselor to other gods and played a key role in ensuring cosmic order and justice. Bastet, goddess of cats, protection, and motherhood, was particularly revered in certain regions and demonstrated the localized character of religious practice in ancient Egypt. Anubis, god of embalming and the afterlife, played a crucial role in funerary rites and emphasized the Egyptian focus on the journey into the afterlife. Khnum, a ram-headed god, is believed to have shaped humans on a potter's wheel, emphasizing the creative power of the divine in shaping life.

The Egyptian pantheon wasn't a static structure; the relative importance and roles of different gods varied over time and across different regions. Local cults and regional variations resulted in a diverse range of beliefs and practices. Certain deities gained prominence in specific periods or locations, highlighting the fluidity of the religious system and its adaptability to changing societal needs and circumstances. The interconnection between gods and the fluidity of their roles reflect the Egyptian understanding of the interconnectedness of the natural world and the dynamism of life and death. The constant interplay between these deities mirrored the complexities of the human experience, demonstrating the challenges and opportunities present in navigating life's uncertainties.

The beliefs and practices surrounding these deities were deeply integrated into all aspects of ancient Egyptian life. Religious rituals, festivals, and funerary practices were meticulously observed and deeply symbolic, underscoring the importance of maintaining harmony between the divine and human realms. The intricate burial practices, with their elaborate tombs and extensive preparation of the deceased, reflect the profound Egyptian belief in the afterlife and the continued existence of the soul. The Book of the Dead, a collection of spells and prayers intended to aid the deceased on their journey to the afterlife, provides insights into the rich and complex beliefs surrounding death and the soul. The Book of the Dead's extensive spells and prayers illustrate the Egyptians' deep engagement with their religious beliefs and their determination to navigate the transition to the next life successfully.

The Egyptian pantheon provided a framework for understanding the world, its origins, and its cyclical nature. The narratives surrounding the gods offered explanations for natural phenomena, provided moral guidance, and offered comfort in the face of death and uncertainty. The system, while seemingly complex, allowed for a deep engagement with spiritual meaning and a coherent worldview that encompassed the entire spectrum of human experience, from birth to death and beyond. It also highlighted the deep intertwining of religious beliefs with political power, with the pharaohs claiming divine authority to legitimize their rule. This interplay between religion and politics served to consolidate social order and reinforce the stability of Egyptian society. The enduring legacy of the Egyptian pantheon, evident in the surviving art, architecture, and texts, provides a rich source of information about ancient Egyptian beliefs and the human quest for understanding the mysteries of life and death. The lasting influence of these beliefs and their adaptability to changing circumstances demonstrate the power and resilience of religious traditions in shaping cultures and societies.

The Concept of Brahman and the Hindu Deities

The Hindu understanding of the divine differs significantly from the polytheistic systems previously examined. While a vast and diverse pantheon of deities populates Hindu mythology, these figures are not considered independent, rivalrous entities in the same way as, for example, the Olympian gods. Instead, they are understood as manifestations or aspects (śakti) of a single, ultimate reality known as Brahman. Brahman is not easily defined; it transcends human comprehension and encompasses all that is, was, and will be. It is the absolute, the unchanging, the source and substance of all existence. It is often described using negations – not this, not that – because any positive attribute would necessarily limit its infinite nature. This concept bears a fascinating resemblance to the Neoplatonic concept of the One, the ultimate source of all being, which influenced later philosophical schools within Hinduism.

The relationship between Brahman and the Hindu deities is often compared to the relationship between the ocean and its waves. The ocean represents Brahman – the boundless, eternal reality. The waves, constantly forming and dissolving, represent the deities – temporary manifestations of Brahman's energy and power. Each deity embodies specific aspects or qualities of Brahman, offering a more accessible and relatable representation of the ultimate reality to human understanding. This does not imply that the deities are illusions; they are profoundly real and powerful, but their reality is contingent upon, and ultimately derived from, Brahman. They are expressions of Brahman's dynamic power, its creativity, its destructive force, and its sustaining presence in the universe.

The concept of Brahman as the ultimate reality has profound implications for Hindu cosmology and soteriology (the study of salvation). The universe, in all its diversity and complexity, is considered a manifestation of Brahman, arising from and ultimately returning to it. The cycle of creation, preservation, and destruction (samsara) is understood as a continuous process of manifestation and reabsorption, governed by the rhythmic interplay of divine energies. This cyclical view stands in contrast to the linear narratives of creation found in many Abrahamic traditions.

Within the Hindu pantheon, several major deities stand out, each representing unique aspects of Brahman's power and nature. Brahma, the creator god, is often depicted as the first being to emerge from Brahman, tasked with bringing the universe into existence. His role is primarily that of creation, shaping the cosmos according to a divine plan. However, Brahma's prominence in popular worship is significantly less than that of Vishnu and Shiva. This relative lack of emphasis reflects the complex interplay of theological ideas and devotional practices that have shaped Hinduism over millennia. Some schools of thought even emphasize the role of Brahman itself as the ultimate creator, bypassing the intermediary role of Brahma altogether.

Vishnu, the preserver god, embodies the sustaining and nurturing aspects of Brahman. Often depicted with multiple arms and holding various symbolic objects, Vishnu's role is to maintain cosmic order and protect the universe from chaos and destruction. He is frequently portrayed descending to earth in various avatars (incarnations), intervening in human affairs to restore dharma (righteousness) and vanquish evil. These avatars, such as Rama and Krishna, are significant figures in Hindu epic literature and devotional traditions, offering relatable models of virtue and spiritual aspiration. Each avatar showcases Vishnu's adaptability, demonstrating his ability to manifest in various forms to meet the specific needs of a particular time and place.

Shiva, the destroyer god, represents the transformative and regenerative aspects of Brahman. While his name often translates to "the destroyer," his function is not simply to annihilate but to dissolve and transform, making way for new creation. His role is vital to the cyclical nature of existence, ensuring that the universe is not stagnant but constantly renewed and evolving. Shiva is often depicted with a third eye, signifying his penetrating insight and transformative power. The destructive aspect is not viewed negatively but as a necessary step in the cosmic cycle, clearing away the old to make space for the new. His consort, Parvati (also known by various other names, such as Durga and Kali), represents the dynamic power of creation and destruction, highlighting the interconnectedness of these seemingly opposing forces.

The interaction between these three major deities, Brahma, Vishnu, and Shiva, highlights the multifaceted nature of Brahman. They are not viewed as rivals but as complementary aspects of the ultimate reality, each playing a crucial role in maintaining the cosmic balance and order. Their roles often overlap, illustrating the subtle and interwoven nature of creation, preservation, and destruction within the Hindu worldview. The understanding of these interactions moves beyond a simple tripartite division to a more nuanced, dynamic interplay of divine energies. Different schools of Hindu thought may emphasize one deity over another, but this does not negate the fundamental underlying unity of Brahman.

Beyond the principal triad, a vast pantheon of other deities enriches the Hindu landscape. These gods and goddesses, often associated with specific aspects of nature, human activities, or specific regions, embody further facets of Brahman's power and grace. Ganesha, the elephant-headed god, is revered as the remover of obstacles and the patron of new beginnings. Lakshmi, the goddess of wealth and prosperity, represents abundance and good fortune. Saraswati, the goddess of knowledge and wisdom, is worshipped as the patron of learning and arts. These and countless other deities demonstrate the adaptability of the Hindu worldview to encompass a wide range of human experiences and aspirations. Their worship provides various paths to spiritual realization and connection with the divine, emphasizing the rich and diverse nature of Hindu religious practice.

The multiplicity of deities within Hinduism does not contradict the concept of Brahman. Instead, it enriches and contextualizes it, providing a multifaceted representation of the ultimate reality. Each deity represents a specific lens through which to perceive the infinite and incomprehensible nature of Brahman. The diversity of Hindu deities reflects the diversity of human experience, offering devotees diverse pathways to connect with the divine and find meaning in their lives. The worship of these deities, through rituals, prayers, and devotional practices, serves as a means of realizing the ultimate reality of Brahman.

Furthermore, the stories and myths associated with these deities play a crucial role in shaping Hindu beliefs and practices. The epics, such as the Ramayana and the Mahabharata, are filled with narratives that illuminate the complex relationship between humans and the divine. These epics explore themes of dharma, karma, reincarnation, and the pursuit of liberation (moksha). They provide moral guidance, illustrate the consequences of human actions, and offer hope in the face of suffering. The narratives often showcase the triumph of good over evil, reinforcing the importance of virtuous conduct and ethical living. The stories serve not simply as entertainment, but as powerful vehicles for transmitting religious and philosophical ideas across generations.

The Hindu worldview, with its emphasis on Brahman and its diverse manifestations in the form of deities, offers a rich tapestry of religious thought and practice. The concept of Brahman, while challenging to grasp fully, provides a unifying principle that binds together the diverse pantheon of Hindu gods and goddesses. The multiplicity of deities does not imply polytheism in the classical sense, but rather, represents a multifaceted reflection of the ultimate, ineffable reality. The interplay between Brahman and its manifestations offers a profound understanding of the divine and its relationship with the human experience. The constant interplay and interaction between these deities within the cosmic order are a mirror reflecting the multifaceted and nuanced nature of the human experience. The continued devotion and worship of these figures demonstrate the enduring power of the Hindu worldview in shaping beliefs and practices, continuing to influence lives across centuries and cultures. The resilience and adaptability of this religious system emphasize the ongoing search for meaning and purpose within the human condition, mirroring themes explored across various religious traditions. The deep engagement with spiritual meaning and the consistent efforts to navigate life's complexities offer a fascinating comparative element with other ancient belief systems.

The Monotheistic God of the Abrahamic Traditions

The transition from the polytheistic or henotheistic frameworks of ancient religions to the rigorously monotheistic God of the Abrahamic traditions represents a profound shift in religious thought. While echoes of earlier cosmogonies and mythological narratives can be found within Abrahamic scriptures, the concept of a singular, transcendent, and all-powerful God stands in stark contrast to the multifaceted pantheons previously examined. This singular deity is not simply one god among many; rather, it is the sole creator, sustainer, and judge of all existence, possessing absolute sovereignty and transcending the limitations of the physical world.

Judaism, the oldest of the Abrahamic faiths, establishes the foundational concept of this singular God. The Hebrew Bible, or Tanakh, emphasizes God's covenant with Abraham, Isaac, and Jacob, highlighting a personal and relational aspect of divinity. This covenant establishes a unique relationship between God and the chosen people, Israel, bestowing upon them both blessings and responsibilities. God is depicted as both creator and lawgiver, revealing his will through the Torah, the first five books of the Bible. The commandments within the Torah provide a moral and ethical framework for Jewish life, underscoring the importance of justice, righteousness, and compassion. While acknowledging God's power and transcendence, Jewish tradition also emphasizes his immanence – his presence and active involvement in the world and the lives of his people. The concept of "Shekhinah," often translated as the divine presence or glory, reflects this immanence, suggesting God's intimate connection with creation. The frequent anthropomorphic descriptions of God in the Hebrew Bible, while often interpreted symbolically, also highlight a certain accessibility and relational aspect of divinity, a quality that contrasts significantly with the impersonal and often unknowable nature of Brahman in Hinduism, for instance.

The development of Jewish theology over centuries further refined the understanding of God. Philosophical schools, such as the Rabbinic tradition, explored the attributes of God, grappling with concepts such as God's unity, omnipotence, omniscience, and omnibenevolence. The challenge of reconciling God's seemingly contradictory attributes – his justice and mercy, his power and compassion – became a central theme in Jewish theological discourse, leading to complex and nuanced interpretations. The ongoing debate surrounding free will versus predestination, for example, illustrates the ongoing attempts to fully comprehend the nature and actions of the divine within a monotheistic framework.

Christianity inherited the Jewish concept of a single God, but introduced the pivotal concept of the Trinity – the belief in one God existing in three co-equal, co-eternal persons: the Father, the Son (Jesus Christ), and the Holy Spirit. This doctrine significantly expanded and nuanced the understanding of the monotheistic God. The incarnation of God in the person of Jesus Christ, his crucifixion, and his resurrection form the cornerstone of Christian faith. This concept of a God who actively participates in human history, suffering alongside humanity, and ultimately offering salvation through sacrifice, stands as a unique theological development within Abrahamic traditions. The New Testament emphasizes the love and grace of God, emphasizing a personal relationship with the divine made possible through faith in Christ. The concept of salvation, the redemption from sin and reconciliation with God, is central to Christian theology, a focus that differentiates it sharply from the soteriological goals found in other religious systems, like the pursuit of moksha in Hinduism or nirvana in Buddhism.

Christian theology, like Jewish theology, has witnessed diverse interpretations and developments throughout history. Different theological schools and denominations offer varying perspectives on the nature of God, the relationship between God and humanity, and the path to salvation. The debates surrounding grace versus works, predestination versus free will, and the nature of the sacraments all showcase the richness and complexity of Christian theological thought. The diversity of Christian interpretations further highlights the ongoing human effort to comprehend the divine within this particular monotheistic framework. The ongoing dialogues within Christianity, reflecting upon the nature and actions of this single, transcendent, and yet personally involved God, continues to shape this religious tradition's evolving understanding of the divine.

Islam, the youngest of the Abrahamic faiths, shares a strong foundation with Judaism and Christianity in its belief in one God, Allah. The Quran, the holy book of Islam, unequivocally proclaims the absolute oneness of God, rejecting any form of polytheism or idolatry. Allah is depicted as the all-powerful, all-knowing, and all-merciful creator of the universe, the ultimate judge, and the source of all goodness. Islam emphasizes the absolute sovereignty of God, highlighting his complete control over all aspects of creation. The five pillars of Islam – the declaration of faith (Shahada), prayer (Salat), charity (Zakat), fasting (Sawm), and pilgrimage (Hajj) – provide a structured framework for Muslim life, demonstrating the practical application of faith in daily life. The Islamic concept of God focuses on his transcendence, his power, and his justice, while also emphasizing his mercy and compassion. Similar to Judaism, Islamic theology also engages with intricate questions about free will, predestination, and divine attributes, leading to a complex and nuanced understanding of the divine. The ongoing development of Islamic jurisprudence (Fiqh) and theology (Kalam) further demonstrates the continuous engagement with the complexities of understanding this single, all-powerful God and his relationship with humanity.

The concept of prophecy plays a significant role in all three Abrahamic traditions, highlighting the ongoing communication between God and humanity. In Judaism, the prophets conveyed God's messages to his people, calling them to repentance and righteousness. In Christianity, Jesus Christ is considered the ultimate prophet and the Son of God, embodying God's message of love and redemption. In Islam, Muhammad is considered the final prophet, receiving the divine revelation of the Quran. The prophetic tradition underlines the ongoing interaction between the transcendent God and the human world, highlighting the dynamic relationship between the divine and the human experience. This concept of divinely-inspired messages, interpreted and reinterpreted over centuries, contributes to the complexity and ongoing evolution of each religious tradition's understanding of the divine.

While sharing fundamental beliefs in a single, all-powerful God, the Abrahamic faiths also demonstrate significant differences in their theological interpretations and practices. These differences, however, do not negate the underlying unity of the monotheistic concept of God. Instead, they enrich and contextualize this concept, revealing its adaptability and capacity to inspire diverse forms of religious expression and experience. The ongoing debates and dialogues within each tradition demonstrate a continuous struggle to fully comprehend the divine within the constraints of human understanding. The shared core belief in a singular, transcendent God, however, provides a powerful testament to the enduring human search for meaning and purpose, a theme that connects the Abrahamic traditions to the broader spectrum of religious experience throughout history and across cultures. The enduring appeal of monotheism, with its focus on a single, powerful, and personally involved God, continues to profoundly shape ethical frameworks, social structures, and personal lives, reflecting the powerful influence of this belief system on societies across millennia. The exploration of this singular concept of God, therefore, remains crucial in understanding the major religious developments of the past and their ongoing impact on the present.

Comparing Divine Figures Different Expressions of the Divine

The preceding chapters have explored a diverse array of divine figures and deities from various ancient religious traditions. From the Olympian gods of ancient Greece to the multifaceted pantheon of ancient Egypt, from the compassionate bodhisattvas of Buddhism to the singular, transcendent God of Abrahamic faiths, the ways in which humanity has conceived and represented the divine are strikingly varied. Yet, beneath the surface of these diverse expressions, intriguing parallels and common threads emerge, offering insights into the enduring human quest for understanding the ultimate reality.

One significant point of comparison lies in the anthropomorphic tendencies evident in many religious traditions. The gods of ancient Greece, for instance, were frequently depicted with human-like qualities, strengths, and weaknesses. Zeus, the king of the gods, was known for his power and authority but also for his infidelity and volatile temper. Similarly, the Egyptian gods, while often possessing unique animalistic or hybrid forms, also exhibited human emotions, motivations, and interpersonal dynamics. Ra, the sun god, was revered for his benevolent power, but also portrayed as engaged in conflicts and struggles with other deities. This anthropomorphism, while seemingly simplistic, served a crucial function: it provided a relatable framework for understanding and interacting with the divine. By ascribing human traits to the gods, ancient cultures made the seemingly distant and incomprehensible concepts of divine power and agency more accessible and comprehensible to the average person. This was particularly critical in societies where religious practices played a central role in daily life, shaping social structures, laws, and even agricultural cycles. The relatable nature of the gods instilled faith and fostered community cohesion by allowing individuals to view the divine as something intimately involved with the human world, not an entirely separate and unknowable entity.

This contrast sharply with the concept of Brahman in Hinduism. Brahman, the ultimate reality and ground of being, is often characterized as impersonal, transcendent, and beyond human comprehension. While Brahman is the source of all creation and the ultimate truth, it lacks the personal characteristics and easily relatable attributes typically found in the anthropomorphic depictions of Greek and Egyptian gods. This distinction reflects a fundamental difference in the philosophical and spiritual approaches of these religious traditions. The Greek and Egyptian polytheistic models tended to emphasize the gods' interaction with humanity, whereas the Hindu concept of Brahman focuses on a transcendental reality that is both immanent and beyond human understanding. The path to understanding Brahman requires a significant spiritual journey and often involves practices like meditation, yoga, and selfless service. The attainment of moksha, liberation from the cycle of reincarnation, is the ultimate goal.

Buddhism, while sharing some cosmological similarities with Hinduism, presents a different perspective on the divine. Buddhist thought typically avoids the concept of a creator god in the traditional sense. Instead, it focuses on the Buddha as an enlightened being, a model for others to follow on the path to enlightenment. The concept of nirvana, the cessation of suffering and the attainment of ultimate peace, serves as the central goal of Buddhist practice, which often includes meditation, mindfulness, and ethical conduct. While compassion and wisdom are often personified as divine attributes associated with bodhisattvas, these are not understood as separate gods but as qualities to be cultivated within oneself.

The Abrahamic traditions, as discussed earlier, present a radically different perspective. The concept of a singular, transcendent God, all-powerful, omniscient, and omnibenevolent, represents a profound shift in religious thought. This monotheistic God is not simply one god among many but the sole creator, sustainer, and judge of all existence. While the anthropomorphic descriptions of God are present in the scriptures of these traditions, they are generally interpreted symbolically, representing certain facets of the divine without implying literal physical attributes. The focus in these faiths is on the relationship between God and humanity, often emphasizing divine grace, mercy, and justice. The emphasis on covenant, divine law, and the prophetic tradition highlights the ongoing communication and interaction between the divine and humanity.

A further area of comparison concerns the role of divine intervention in the human world. In many polytheistic religions, gods actively intervened in human affairs, influencing events, battles, and the lives of individuals. This intervention was often seen as direct and immediate, reflecting the intimate connection between the gods and humanity. In contrast, the Abrahamic conception of God often involves a more indirect or subtle form of divine intervention, frequently working through natural processes, human agency, or miraculous events. This nuanced approach to divine intervention reflects a balance between divine sovereignty and human free will, a crucial element in the theological discourse of these traditions.

The diversity of divine figures and conceptions across cultures and time periods underscores the multifaceted nature of the human experience of the divine. The very act of attempting to define and represent the ultimate reality is inherently challenging, leading to a vast array of interpretations and representations. The common threads among these various representations—the search for meaning, the desire for connection with something greater than oneself, the longing for justice, compassion, and ultimate truth—point to fundamental aspects of the human condition. These shared experiences and aspirations, expressed through diverse religious systems and conceptions of the divine, illustrate the enduring power of religion to shape individual lives and cultures. The continuing exploration and comparison of these different approaches to the divine, therefore, remains a critical undertaking in the study of comparative religion and the broader understanding of human civilization.

Furthermore, the very act of comparing and contrasting these diverse divine figures necessitates a critical approach, avoiding any simplistic judgments of superiority or inferiority. Each religious tradition, with its unique pantheon or conception of divinity, has served to provide meaning, purpose, and social cohesion for its adherents. Recognizing the richness and complexity of each tradition is paramount, highlighting their importance within their respective historical and cultural contexts. The parallels and contrasts between these diverse expressions of the divine provide valuable insights into the evolution of religious thought, the human capacity for creativity and spiritual expression, and the enduring quest for understanding the ultimate nature of reality. The diverse responses to this quest, spanning millennia and diverse cultures, create a rich tapestry of human experience. By studying these diverse expressions carefully and comparatively, we gain a deeper understanding not only of the history of religions but also of the enduring human search for meaning and purpose in a complex and often chaotic world. The study of comparative religion allows us to appreciate the diversity of human spiritual expression, while simultaneously recognizing the underlying unity of the human experience itself. This unity, expressed through the shared themes of love, compassion, justice, and the search for ultimate truth, underlies the diverse expressions of the divine across cultures and time periods. The task of understanding and interpreting these expressions continues to challenge and inspire scholars and individuals alike, underscoring the enduring relevance of comparative religion in our ever-changing world. The continuing study of these religious traditions, therefore, remains crucial for deepening our understanding of human history, society, and the ongoing quest for meaning that lies at the heart of the human experience. The diverse approaches to understanding and interacting with the divine offer valuable insights into the remarkable ability of humanity to grapple with profound existential questions, developing complex and sophisticated systems of belief and practice to provide structure, meaning, and hope in the face of life's uncertainties.

Exploring the Apocryphal Gospels and Their Significance

The preceding discussion has focused on established canonical texts and their interpretations across diverse religious traditions. However, a crucial aspect of understanding the evolution of religious belief lies in examining the apocryphal and pseudepigraphical literature that often exists alongside canonical texts. These non-canonical writings, while not officially recognized as part of a religion's core scriptures, offer invaluable insights into the broader spectrum of religious thought and practice, particularly in their historical and cultural contexts. This section will delve into the world of the Apocryphal Gospels, a body of texts that offers a fascinating counterpoint to the four canonical Gospels of the New Testament.

The term "Apocrypha" itself carries a complex history. Initially, it simply meant "hidden" or "secret" texts, referring to writings that were not readily available or widely circulated. Over time, the term took on a more negative connotation, often implying that these texts were deemed heretical or unreliable. This negative association, however, often obscures the historical and theological significance of these texts. Many apocryphal writings offer unique perspectives on the life, teachings, and ministry of Jesus, providing glimpses into the diversity of early Christian belief and the evolution of theological interpretations.

The Apocryphal Gospels are not a single unified work, but rather a collection of diverse texts, written over a period of several centuries, and reflecting a range of theological perspectives and literary styles. Their authorship is often uncertain, with many attributed anonymously or to figures who may or may not have actually existed. This anonymity, however, does not necessarily detract from their value, but highlights the dynamic and fluid nature of early Christian thought. These texts were often passed down through oral tradition before being committed to writing, contributing to variations in their content and interpretation across different manuscripts.

The historical context of the Apocryphal Gospels is critical to understanding their content. Many were written in the late 1st century CE and the following centuries, a period marked by significant theological debates and the ongoing development of Christian doctrine. The canonization process of the New Testament itself was a gradual and complex process, involving theological debate and the selection of certain texts while others were excluded. The Apocryphal Gospels often reflect the theological debates and struggles of this formative period, offering insights into perspectives that ultimately were not incorporated into the established canon.

Several factors influenced the exclusion of these texts from the New Testament canon. Some apocryphal gospels contained theological interpretations deemed heretical or contrary to the developing orthodoxy of the early church. Other texts were excluded due to concerns about their authenticity, with questions raised about their authorship and historical accuracy. The inclusion of certain texts and the exclusion of others was a complex process, shaped by theological, social, and political factors, reflecting the power dynamics of the early church itself. It's crucial to avoid seeing this process as a simple matter of truth versus falsehood, but rather as a reflection of the multifaceted evolution of Christian belief and the establishment of orthodox doctrine within a specific historical and cultural context.

Among the most well-known Apocryphal Gospels is the Gospel of Thomas. Unlike the canonical Gospels, which present narrative accounts of Jesus' life and ministry, the Gospel of Thomas is a collection of 114 sayings attributed to Jesus. These sayings often offer a different perspective on Jesus' teachings, focusing on gnostic themes and emphasizing the importance of inner knowledge and spiritual enlightenment. Some scholars suggest that the Gospel of Thomas represents a very early form of Christian tradition, possibly predating the canonical Gospels. Others posit it as a later gnostic interpretation. Regardless of its exact date and origins, the Gospel of Thomas provides a valuable glimpse into early Christian gnostic thought. Gnosticism, a diverse body of religious thought, emphasized a sharp distinction between the material world, seen as evil, and the spiritual world, considered divine. Gnostic Christians believed that true salvation lay in achieving gnosis, or spiritual knowledge, leading to liberation from the material realm.

The Gospel of Peter is another notable example of an Apocryphal Gospel, offering a unique account of Jesus' crucifixion and resurrection. This gospel expands on the canonical narratives, adding details and perspectives that differ from the canonical accounts. In particular, it portrays the crucifixion in a somewhat different light, emphasizing the role of the Jewish authorities and portraying Pilate as more sympathetic to Jesus than in the canonical Gospels. The Gospel of Peter also contains a description of the resurrection that differs from the accounts in the canonical Gospels, which further highlights the diversity of early Christian interpretations of these central events. The differing depictions of Pilate also underscore the socio-political realities and anxieties that shaped the early Church, highlighting the significance of early Christian identity in relation to Roman governance.

The Gospel of Judas is perhaps the most controversial of the Apocryphal Gospels. Discovered in the 1970s, this text presents a radically different portrayal of Judas Iscariot, portraying him not as a betrayer, but as a disciple acting on Jesus' instructions. This interpretation challenges the traditional understanding of Judas' role in the crucifixion, leading to considerable debate among scholars and theologians. The Gospel of Judas reflects a particular Gnostic perspective, emphasizing secret knowledge and the importance of spiritual enlightenment over outward conformity. Its discovery, however, sparked significant debate on its historicity, authenticity and its place within the larger history of early Christian beliefs. The text's significance lies primarily in its illumination of the diverse range of interpretations of Judas' role and actions, highlighting a radical departure from mainstream Christian thought and providing a contrasting perspective on the crucifixion narrative.

The Infancy Gospel of Thomas provides a different perspective. It's not focused on the adult Jesus' ministry, but instead presents a collection of stories about Jesus' childhood. These stories, often miraculous and sometimes violent, are not found in the canonical Gospels and demonstrate a range of literary and theological styles common in the wider religious landscape of the period. These narratives often reveal the cultural anxieties and expectations associated with raising a child perceived to be extraordinary or possessing special powers. The Infancy Gospel is a compelling illustration of how early Christians envisioned Jesus' childhood and how this vision varied across diverse communities.

The significance of these Apocryphal Gospels extends far beyond their mere existence. They provide valuable insights into the complexities of early Christian thought and the multifaceted ways in which the life and teachings of Jesus were understood and interpreted during the formative years of Christianity. The diversity of these texts highlights the fact that early Christianity was not a monolithic entity, but rather a collection of diverse communities with varying theological perspectives and interpretations. Studying them allows for a richer and more nuanced understanding of the intellectual and theological landscapes of the early Christian world. The contrasts between the apocryphal and canonical Gospels illuminate not just the doctrinal disputes but also the socio-political realities shaping these narratives.

Furthermore, the Apocryphal Gospels serve as a reminder of the importance of considering the historical context in which religious texts are produced and interpreted. The canonical Gospels themselves were selected from a much larger body of early Christian writings, and the criteria for their selection were complex and influenced by a variety of factors. Understanding the historical reasons for the inclusion or exclusion of certain texts is essential for a more comprehensive understanding of the evolution of Christian belief. The apocryphal gospels serve as a critical counterpoint, reminding us that the canonical texts represent only one strand within a broader tapestry of early Christian beliefs. The ongoing study of these texts illuminates the nuanced and multifaceted early history of Christianity, enriching our understanding of the various interpretations of scripture, theology, and practice. The diversity of these texts, while often contradictory in nature, demonstrates the vibrancy and dynamism of religious and philosophical thought in the ancient world, highlighting both commonalities and radical differences in theological approaches.

Finally, the study of the Apocryphal Gospels encourages a critical approach to the interpretation of religious texts, urging readers to question assumptions and engage with diverse perspectives. By comparing and contrasting these texts with the canonical Gospels, we can gain a deeper appreciation for the complexities of religious history and the ongoing evolution of religious belief. These texts are not merely historical artifacts; they are windows into a complex intellectual and spiritual world, revealing the diversity of thought and the challenges of constructing and maintaining orthodoxy within any religious tradition. The investigation of these texts, therefore, is not merely an academic pursuit, but an essential step towards a more comprehensive understanding of the historical development and continuing evolution of religious belief. Their study encourages a critical engagement with sources, promoting a nuanced perspective on the complexities of religious history and the ongoing evolution of faith itself. Ultimately, the apocryphal gospels encourage a deeper understanding of the human quest for meaning and the diverse ways this quest has been expressed throughout history.

The Dead Sea Scrolls and Their Contribution to Our Understanding of Judaism

The exploration of apocryphal texts thus far has illuminated the diverse and often contested landscapes of early Christianity. However, the richness of extra-canonical literature extends beyond the New Testament. Turning our attention to Judaism, we find a similarly vibrant and complex tapestry of writings, perhaps none more significant than the Dead Sea Scrolls. Discovered in 1946-47 in eleven caves near Qumran, on the northwest shore of the Dead Sea, these ancient manuscripts offer an unparalleled glimpse into Jewish religious life during the Second Temple period (roughly 515 BCE – 70 CE), a period bridging the gap between the Old Testament and the emergence of Rabbinic Judaism. Their discovery revolutionized our understanding of Second Temple Judaism, challenging long-held assumptions and providing crucial context for the development of subsequent Jewish traditions.

The sheer quantity and variety of the Dead Sea Scrolls are astonishing. The scrolls encompass a wide range of texts, including biblical books, commentaries on biblical books, sectarian writings, prayers, hymns, calendars, and legal documents. The biblical texts include fragments of virtually every book of the Hebrew Bible, some representing earlier versions than those found in the Masoretic Text, the standard Hebrew Bible used today. The discovery of these variant readings has been invaluable in textual criticism, allowing scholars to reconstruct the history of the biblical text and to trace its evolution over centuries. The differences, while often subtle, sometimes reveal significant variations in wording, suggesting different scribal traditions and offering potential insights into the development of the biblical canon.

The commentaries, known as pesharim, offer particularly fascinating insights into the religious and intellectual world of the Qumran community. These commentaries interpret biblical texts in light of the community’s own beliefs and experiences, often allegorically linking biblical events to contemporary events and situations. For instance, the pesher on Habakkuk interprets the prophet's lamentations as a prophecy of the community's struggles against the "Kittim" (often interpreted as a Hellenistic power, possibly the Romans), framing their own sectarian conflict within a broader biblical narrative. This practice reveals a distinctive hermeneutical approach, emphasizing the ongoing relevance of Scripture to the present moment, and providing valuable data about the community’s self-understanding within the broader historical context of Second Temple Judea.

Beyond the biblical commentaries, the Dead Sea Scrolls contain a wealth of sectarian literature, offering unique insights into the beliefs and practices of the Qumran community itself. These documents reveal a group with distinct beliefs and practices that differed significantly from those of mainstream Second Temple Judaism. The Community Rule, or *Ḥeḳḳet ha-Yaḥad* , outlines the community's rules and regulations, detailing its communal organization, its strict adherence to purity laws, and its emphasis on communal life and shared resources. The Manual of Discipline, another crucial document, describes the community's structure, rituals, and social norms, shedding light on their rigorous lifestyle and their commitment to communal living. These texts provide detailed information about aspects of their daily life, from dietary laws to communal worship, offering a compelling picture of a distinctly ascetic and intensely communal society.

The scrolls' liturgical texts further deepen our understanding of Qumran's religious practices. Hymns and prayers discovered among the scrolls reveal a profound piety and a deep engagement with the divine. These liturgical texts often reflect a messianic expectation, anticipating the arrival of a divinely appointed leader who would bring about a new era of righteousness. This expectation, expressed through numerous hymns and prophecies, provides a unique window into the varied messianic expectations prevalent within Second Temple Judaism, underscoring the diversity of beliefs and interpretations within the wider Jewish religious landscape.

The calendar documents discovered among the scrolls are particularly significant, shedding light on the community's meticulous observance of the Jewish calendar and their unique reckoning of time. These documents provide detailed information about the calculation of the Sabbath and festivals, revealing a system that differed somewhat from that used by other Jewish groups during the Second Temple period. This information contributes significantly to the understanding of how Jewish calendrical systems were constructed and maintained across different Jewish communities, highlighting the complexities and diversity of Jewish practice across various regions and groups.

The presence of non-religious texts among the scrolls, such as legal documents and letters, adds further context to the lives of the Qumran community. These documents provide everyday details about their economic activities, their social interactions, and their concerns, offering a glimpse beyond their religious beliefs and practices. These texts reveal the mundane realities that framed their daily life, the complexities of their interactions with the wider world, and their practical considerations beyond their religious worldview.

The identity of the Qumran community remains a subject of scholarly debate. While widely believed to be associated with the Essenes, a Jewish sect mentioned by ancient historians like Philo of Alexandria and Pliny the Elder, the exact nature of their relationship is still debated. The scrolls themselves offer clues, but definitive answers remain elusive. The sectarian literature emphasizes the community's strict adherence to the Law, its communal lifestyle, and its belief in a coming apocalyptic event. These characteristics align with some of the descriptions of the Essenes by ancient historians, although they also diverge in certain aspects. Ongoing scholarship carefully analyzes linguistic features and ritual practices to continue to refine our understanding of the Qumran community's identity, its relationship to other Jewish groups, and its position within the broader context of Second Temple Judaism.

The significance of the Dead Sea Scrolls cannot be overstated. They offer an unparalleled window into the diversity of Jewish religious life during the Second Temple period, revealing a complex spectrum of beliefs, practices, and interpretations. Their impact on biblical studies, Jewish history, and religious studies is profound. The scrolls' contribution to textual criticism has been essential in refining our understanding of the Hebrew Bible's textual transmission. They also offer invaluable insights into the development of Jewish religious thought, demonstrating the intellectual and theological ferment of the period.

Furthermore, the Dead Sea Scrolls challenge simplistic narratives of the development of Judaism. They demonstrate a religious landscape far more diverse and nuanced than previously imagined, demonstrating the existence of significant sectarian movements with distinct beliefs and practices. The scrolls underscore that early Judaism was not a monolithic entity but a dynamic and evolving religious tradition with considerable internal diversity and debate. This multiplicity of beliefs and practices complicates previous models of Jewish history, forcing a more critical evaluation of traditional assumptions about the evolution of Judaism and its relation to other religious movements of the Second Temple period.

The Scrolls also challenge assumptions about the relationship between the various Jewish groups of that era and the broader historical context in which they existed. They reveal interactions with other communities, the realities of political and social influence, and the complexities of identity formation and sectarian conflict. The texts' geopolitical context, reflecting the influences of various empires and cultural groups on Judea, illuminates the significance of power dynamics and socio-political influences on religious practices and beliefs.

Finally, the Dead Sea Scrolls serve as a powerful reminder of the importance of studying religious texts within their historical context. By understanding the historical, social, and political factors that shaped the Qumran community, we gain a richer appreciation of the beliefs and practices reflected in their writings. Their significance lies not only in the content of the texts themselves but also in the insights they offer into the historical, social, and intellectual context in which they were produced. This historical context significantly shapes our interpretation of the texts and enhances our understanding of the historical development of religious thought. Understanding this context is crucial to appropriately interpreting the scrolls’ contents and avoiding anachronistic readings.

In conclusion, the Dead Sea Scrolls stand as a monumental discovery in the field of religious studies and ancient history.

Their extraordinary preservation has yielded an invaluable collection of documents that illuminate the complexities of Second Temple Judaism in unprecedented detail. Their diverse content, ranging from biblical texts and commentaries to sectarian writings and liturgical materials, provides an unparalleled window into the richness and diversity of Jewish religious life during a pivotal period in its history. Their significance continues to resonate with scholars today, challenging long-held assumptions and deepening our understanding of the ongoing evolution of Judaism and its relationship to the wider ancient world. The ongoing scholarly investigation of the Dead Sea Scrolls promises to continue to yield significant insights into the evolution of Jewish faith and practice for many years to come.

The Kybalion and Hermeticism Ancient Wisdom Traditions

Having delved into the fascinating world of apocryphal texts within Judaism and early Christianity, our exploration of lesser-known traditions now turns to Hermeticism and its most widely known modern expression, the *Kybalion* . Hermeticism, a complex and multifaceted philosophical and religious system, boasts an ancient and enigmatic history, its origins shrouded in mystery and debated by scholars for centuries. While precise origins are elusive, its influences are undeniably ancient, drawing from Egyptian, Greek, and possibly even earlier Mesopotamian sources. The name itself derives from Hermes Trismegistus, a legendary figure often depicted as a Greco-Egyptian sage who is credited with a vast body of writings encompassing philosophy, theology, alchemy, and magic. It's crucial to note that no historical evidence confirms the existence of a single individual named Hermes Trismegistus; rather, the name represents a collective body of wisdom attributed to a mythical figurehead.

The core tenets of Hermeticism center on a few key principles that, although expressed in various ways throughout its history, reveal a consistent underlying philosophy. These include the profound belief in the interconnectedness of all things – a concept frequently expressed as the "correspondence" or "as above, so below" principle. This principle highlights the mirroring relationship between the macrocosm (the universe) and the microcosm (the individual). What happens in the heavens reflects, in miniature, what happens within a person and vice versa. This idea is not unique to Hermeticism, appearing in various forms across different ancient traditions, but it serves as a cornerstone of Hermetic thought.

Another significant principle is the importance of inner transformation and self-knowledge. Hermetic texts emphasize the power of self-mastery and the cultivation of inner wisdom as a path to spiritual enlightenment and understanding the universe's mysteries. This emphasis on self-discovery resonates with similar themes in various philosophical and religious traditions, suggesting a shared understanding of the human potential for spiritual growth and self-realization. It's essential to emphasize that this pursuit of self-knowledge isn't a purely introspective activity but rather involves a thorough understanding of the universe and one's place within it. This is where the principles of correspondence and analogy play a critical role. By understanding the workings of the cosmos, the Hermetic practitioner seeks to understand themselves and, through self-mastery, influence their environment.

Alchemy, a practice interwoven with Hermetic thought, plays a significant role in understanding the system's core principles. For the Hermeticists, alchemy was not merely a proto-scientific pursuit of transforming base metals into gold; it was a symbolic and spiritual process of inner transformation. The transmutation of lead into gold served as a metaphor for the spiritual journey of self-discovery and self-perfection. The various stages of alchemical processes — calcination, dissolution, separation, conjunction, fermentation, distillation, sublimation, and multiplication — represented the successive stages of spiritual purification and enlightenment. The adept would pass through these stages, symbolically refining their souls and achieving a state of spiritual perfection, much like the transmutation of base metal into gold. This symbolic interpretation demonstrates the Hermetic inclination towards a complex, multi-layered understanding of reality, where physical processes mirror spiritual ones.

The concept of "Mind" also plays a pivotal role in Hermetic philosophy. The Hermetic tradition posits the universe as being fundamentally mental in nature, with "Mind" being the underlying creative force responsible for the manifestation of reality. This concept is closely linked to the idea of the divine Mind or a universal consciousness that permeates all aspects of existence. The individual human mind, in this framework, is a part of this greater Mind, possessing the potential to tap into its creative power. This resonates with pantheistic and panentheistic worldviews, suggesting a strong interconnectedness between the divine and the human consciousness, where the divine is present in, and actively shaping, all of existence. However, it is not to be confused with simple idealism. The Hermetic tradition understands a physical reality to exist and that its structure and function are interwoven with this universal Mind.

The *Kybalion* , a 20th-century text purportedly based on ancient Hermetic principles, codified many of these ideas into a more accessible format. While its authenticity as an ancient text is debatable, it has significantly influenced contemporary understanding of Hermeticism, presenting its core tenets in a clear and concise manner. The *Kybalion* popularized the seven Hermetic principles: Mentalism, Correspondence, Vibration, Polarity, Rhythm, Cause and Effect, and Gender. These principles, while presented as distinct, are interconnected and interwoven, reflecting the holistic and integrated nature of Hermetic thought.

Mentalism, as presented in the *Kybalion* , emphasizes the primacy of the Mind in creation and manifestation. The universe is said to be a mental creation, and the ability to understand and work with this fundamental principle allows for manipulation of reality through focused thought and intent. This idea emphasizes a fundamental connection between mental processes and the physical world, suggesting that thoughts and intentions are not simply mental events, but have the capacity to influence the universe's structure and function.

The principle of Correspondence, already mentioned above, highlights the mirroring relationships between different levels of reality – from the macrocosm to the microcosm, from the physical to the spiritual. The understanding of these correspondences is key to unlocking the mysteries of the universe and achieving a greater comprehension of self and reality.

Vibration posits that everything in the universe is in a state of constant vibration, with different frequencies corresponding to different manifestations of reality. This concept connects the apparently static physical world with the dynamic energy that underpins it. It helps to explain the way reality can be influenced by thought and intention.

Polarity emphasizes the dualistic nature of reality. Every concept has an opposite, and the two are interconnected and interdependent. Understanding this duality is essential for achieving balance and mastering the seeming contradictions of life.

Rhythm describes the ebb and flow of energy and the cyclical nature of existence. Understanding and working with these rhythms is crucial for navigating life's challenges and harnessing its energy effectively.

Cause and Effect is a universal law governing the relationship between actions and consequences. Every action creates a reaction, and understanding this law is crucial for taking responsibility for one's life and achieving desired outcomes.

Gender emphasizes the principle of duality present in all things, not just in the obvious male-female sense, but also encompassing positive and negative, active and passive forces present in all creation. The understanding of these dualities helps to balance opposing forces within the individual and the universe.

The *Kybalion* ’s influence on Western esotericism and the New Thought movement has been significant. Its clear articulation of Hermetic principles made them accessible to a wider audience, leading to their integration into various occult and self-help systems. However, it’s crucial to approach the *Kybalion* with a critical eye, recognizing that while it popularized Hermetic principles, it is not a primary source for understanding the historical development of Hermeticism. Its interpretation and presentation of those ancient principles represent one perspective among many.

The study of Hermeticism and related traditions offers valuable insights into the historical development of Western esoteric thought, its intricate connections to ancient wisdom traditions, and its enduring influence on contemporary spirituality and occult practices. The enduring appeal of Hermetic ideas suggests a deep resonance with fundamental human aspirations for self-understanding, spiritual growth, and a deeper comprehension of the universe's mysteries. Its principles, even if presented through a modern lens as in the *Kybalion* , continue to inspire individuals seeking personal transformation and a deeper connection with the cosmos. The ongoing exploration of these ancient traditions continues to unveil their rich layers of meaning and to illuminate the ongoing human quest for wisdom and understanding.

Exploring Ancient Mesopotamian Religious Texts Beyond the Epic of Gilgamesh

The Epic of Gilgamesh, with its iconic hero grappling with mortality and legacy, often dominates discussions of Mesopotamian religious texts. However, the rich tapestry of Mesopotamian belief extends far beyond this singular narrative. A vast corpus of texts, many fragmentary and obscure, offers glimpses into a complex and multifaceted religious landscape, revealing nuances and variations in belief systems that the Gilgamesh epic, while powerful, cannot fully represent. These lesser-known texts provide a more nuanced understanding of Mesopotamian cosmology, rituals, and the interactions between humans and the divine.

One crucial area to explore is the extensive collection of hymns and prayers dedicated to various Mesopotamian deities. Unlike the narrative structure of the Epic of Gilgamesh, these texts offer direct access to the devotional practices and theological beliefs of the time. Hymns to deities like Ishtar (Inanna), the goddess of love, war, and fertility, reveal her multifaceted nature and the range of emotions and expectations associated with her worship. These hymns frequently depict Ishtar's power and majesty, her role in the cosmos, and her capacity for both creation and destruction. The supplicatory nature of the prayers reveals the anxieties and hopes of the worshippers, who sought Ishtar's favor in various aspects of their lives, from fertility and prosperity to protection in battle. The language used in these hymns, often poetic and evocative, speaks volumes about the emotional intensity of the religious experience in ancient Mesopotamia.

Beyond hymns, a significant body of Mesopotamian religious texts consists of incantations, spells, and rituals aimed at warding off evil, curing illness, and ensuring good fortune. These texts offer invaluable insight into the Mesopotamian understanding of the supernatural world and the methods employed to navigate its capricious forces. The incantations are replete with magical formulas, divine names, and symbolic language, suggesting a deep belief in the power of words and rituals to influence the supernatural realm. Often, these texts mention specific demons or malevolent spirits believed to cause illness or misfortune, providing details about the Mesopotamian understanding of demonic forces and the means of exorcism and protection. The precise rituals, sometimes involving offerings, incantations, and symbolic actions, further illuminate the practical aspects of Mesopotamian religious life. These texts are not merely abstract theological statements; they represent the lived religious experience of the people, detailing their interactions with the world of spirits and their attempts to control or appease supernatural forces.

The "Descent of Ishtar" is a particularly compelling example of a myth beyond the Epic of Gilgamesh. This myth depicts Ishtar's journey to the underworld, her encounter with the Queen of the Dead, and her eventual return to the land of the living. The narrative is rich in symbolism, exploring themes of death, resurrection, and the cyclical nature of life. The myth's structure mirrors the seasonal changes in nature, where Ishtar's descent into the underworld can be interpreted as the winter season and her ascent, the spring. The tale reveals a sophisticated understanding of the relationship between the gods and the natural world, and it showcases the Mesopotamian understanding of the cyclical nature of life and death. Furthermore, the myth serves as a powerful narrative that reinforces the cyclical nature of the universe, emphasizing the inevitability of death but also the possibility of renewal and rebirth. This cyclical understanding profoundly influenced Mesopotamian society's worldview and religious practices.

Another important aspect of Mesopotamian religion that is not always highlighted in the Epic of Gilgamesh is the concept of divine judgment and the afterlife. While Gilgamesh's quest for immortality is central to the epic, other texts offer a more detailed exploration of the Mesopotamian understanding of the afterlife. The "Epic of Erra" recounts the destruction of the world by the god Erra and the subsequent re-establishment of order. This text explores themes of divine justice, chaos, and the fragility of human civilization. The narrative provides insights into the Mesopotamian view of divine power and the consequences of human actions in the eyes of the gods. It also subtly hints at the idea of divine intervention and the possibility of redemption, even after widespread destruction.

Furthermore, numerous omen texts and divinatory practices reveal the Mesopotamian concern with predicting the future and interpreting the will of the gods. These texts describe a wide range of omens, from the behavior of animals to natural phenomena, and their associated interpretations. This emphasis on divination highlights the Mesopotamian belief in the gods' pervasive influence on human affairs and the importance of understanding divine intentions. These omens were carefully recorded and consulted by priests, who played a crucial role in interpreting the will of the gods and advising rulers on matters of state and personal affairs. The elaborate system of divination reflected the Mesopotamian belief in the interconnectedness of the human and divine realms, and the belief that the future was not entirely predetermined but could be influenced by understanding and interpreting divine signs.

Moreover, the study of ancient Mesopotamian legal codes, such as the Code of Hammurabi, sheds light on the intricate relationship between law, religion, and social order. While not strictly religious texts, these codes reflect the religious worldview that underpins Mesopotamian society. Many of the laws reflect the religious beliefs and values of the time, with punishments often invoking divine retribution for transgression. The close connection between law and religion demonstrates the pervasive influence of religious beliefs on everyday life in ancient Mesopotamia, permeating social structures, legal systems, and individual morality. The concept of justice itself was deeply intertwined with the divine, and legal codes served as a practical manifestation of the divine order sought to be maintained in human society.

In conclusion, while the Epic of Gilgamesh provides a captivating narrative window into Mesopotamian beliefs, it represents only a small fraction of the vast and complex religious landscape of ancient Mesopotamia. The wealth of hymns, prayers, incantations, myths, omen texts, and legal codes reveals a rich and nuanced understanding of the Mesopotamian worldview, their interactions with the divine, and the deep integration of religion into their daily lives. The exploration of these lesser-known texts provides a far more comprehensive picture of Mesopotamian religion, moving beyond the heroic narrative of Gilgamesh to encompass the devotional practices, anxieties, hopes, and profound beliefs of a civilization deeply intertwined with the divine. Further research into these fragmentary and often overlooked texts is crucial to gaining a more complete understanding of one of the world's oldest and most influential civilizations. The study of these diverse textual sources allows for a more nuanced and complete comprehension of Mesopotamian religious thought, offering valuable insights into the human condition and the enduring quest for meaning and purpose across vastly different cultural and temporal contexts. The multifaceted nature of Mesopotamian religion, as revealed through these diverse texts, highlights the complexity and dynamism of ancient religious systems and their profound influence on shaping societies and cultures.

The Value of Studying Apocryphal and LesserKnown Texts

The preceding exploration of Mesopotamian religious texts, while focusing on some key narratives and genres, has only scratched the surface of the rich tapestry of beliefs and practices that shaped this ancient civilization. To gain a truly comprehensive understanding, we must turn our attention to the apocryphal and lesser-known texts that often lie neglected in the shadows of more famous works. The value of studying these texts is multifaceted and profoundly impacts our understanding of ancient religious traditions. Their significance transcends mere academic curiosity; they offer crucial insights into the evolution of religious thought, the diversity of belief systems within a single culture, and the complexities of human interaction with the divine.

Firstly, apocryphal and lesser-known texts often reveal alternative perspectives and interpretations of established narratives. Take, for instance, the numerous variations of creation myths found in ancient cultures. While the Enuma Elish, a Babylonian creation epic, provides one account of the cosmos' origin, other, less-documented accounts may offer subtly different perspectives on the roles of various deities, the process of creation itself, and the relationship between the divine and the earthly realms. These variations, far from being inconsequential, highlight the fluidity and dynamic nature of religious beliefs, suggesting that religious truth was not monolithic but subject to interpretation and reinterpretation over time. The existence of multiple versions of the same story suggests a process of adaptation and innovation within the religious system, responding to changing social and environmental circumstances. Studying these variations allows us to move beyond simplistic narratives of unchanging dogma and to appreciate the organic evolution of religious thought.

Moreover, these overlooked texts frequently unveil details omitted from canonical narratives. The canonical texts, often shaped by later editorial processes or institutional agendas, might present a sanitized or idealized version of religious beliefs and practices. Apocryphal texts, on the other hand, might contain more raw, unfiltered accounts of religious life, including aspects considered taboo or inappropriate for public consumption. These might include details about esoteric rituals, unorthodox interpretations of religious doctrine, or accounts of heretical beliefs that challenged established orthodoxies. Such materials provide invaluable insights into the internal debates, controversies, and complexities that characterized ancient religious landscapes. The study of these marginalized voices offers a more nuanced and accurate picture of the lived religious experiences of ancient peoples, moving beyond the official accounts to capture the diversity of beliefs and practices within a culture.

For example, consider the numerous magical incantations and amulets discovered in ancient Egyptian contexts. While the Book of the Dead offers a structured account of funerary beliefs and practices, the multitude of lesser-known spells and charms reveals a much broader spectrum of magical practices aimed at various aspects of life, from healing and protection to securing love and success. These texts expose a more personal and pragmatic approach to religion, showing how ancient Egyptians utilized religious beliefs and practices to cope with the uncertainties and challenges of daily life. The language, imagery, and rituals employed in these texts often differ significantly from the formal religious texts, suggesting a parallel religious culture thriving alongside the official religious institutions.

Another valuable contribution of apocryphal and lesser-known texts is their potential to illuminate the relationship between different religious traditions. While focusing solely on canonical texts might give the impression of distinct, isolated religious systems, the study of less-known texts can reveal surprising connections and cross-cultural influences. For example, parallels have been drawn between certain motifs and narratives found in the Gnostic Gospels and other religious traditions in the Near East, suggesting a possible interchange of religious ideas and practices across geographical boundaries. This highlights the interconnectedness of ancient religious systems and challenges the notion of rigidly defined religious boundaries. The exchange and adaptation of religious concepts and practices across different cultures reveal a dynamic and evolving religious landscape, constantly shaped by interactions and cross-fertilization.

Furthermore, the study of these texts offers an opportunity to engage with the lived religious experiences of ordinary people, rather than solely focusing on the perspectives of elites or religious leaders. Canonical texts often reflect the official ideology and theology of a particular religious establishment. Apocryphal and lesser-known texts, however, often provide glimpses into the personal beliefs, practices, and interpretations of ordinary individuals, offering a more grassroots perspective on religious life. These may include personal prayers, devotional texts, or accounts of religious experiences that offer a counterpoint to the official narratives.

The study of these texts also encourages a more critical engagement with the historical context in which they were produced. Canonical texts are often seen as timeless and unchanging, but a critical analysis reveals that they are products of their time and place, reflecting the social, political, and cultural circumstances in which they were created. Studying apocryphal and lesser-known texts offers a deeper understanding of the historical conditions that shaped the development of religious ideas and practices, revealing the influence of factors such as political power, social structures, and cultural exchange.

Beyond specific textual examples, the very act of seeking out and analyzing these marginalized texts embodies a crucial methodological principle in the study of religion: the recognition of the incompleteness of the available evidence. No archive is complete. Every collection of texts reflects a process of selection, preservation, and transmission that is inherently biased. By actively seeking out the fragmentary, the incomplete, and the overlooked, we acknowledge the limitations of our sources and approach the study of ancient religion with a greater degree of humility and critical awareness. We avoid the pitfalls of constructing narratives based on an incomplete picture, recognizing the gaps and silences in the historical record and the potential for misinterpretation.

The comparative study of religion is enriched by a deliberate effort to include these marginalized voices. Focusing solely on widely known texts leads to a simplified and potentially distorted understanding of the complexity of religious thought and practice. The inclusion of apocryphal and lesser-known texts serves to broaden our scope, challenge our assumptions, and deepen our understanding of the intricate interplay between religious beliefs, social structures, and cultural contexts in the ancient world.

In conclusion, the value of studying apocryphal and lesser-known texts lies not only in filling gaps in our knowledge but also in fostering a more nuanced, critical, and holistic understanding of ancient religious traditions. These texts provide alternative perspectives, expose overlooked details, illuminate cross-cultural influences, and offer a more grassroots understanding of lived religious experience. By engaging with these often-neglected sources, we broaden our understanding of the human condition and the enduring search for meaning and purpose across vastly different cultural and temporal contexts. The study of these texts is not merely an academic exercise; it is a crucial step towards a richer and more complete appreciation of the religious history of humankind. The persistent quest to unearth, analyze, and interpret these fragments is vital in reconstructing a more accurate and comprehensive understanding of the past, and the human experience that shaped it. Furthermore, this process enhances our ability to interpret the present, recognizing that the themes and struggles reflected in these ancient texts continue to resonate with humanity across millennia.

The Impact of Geography on Religious Beliefs and Practices

The preceding discussion highlighted the importance of considering lesser-known texts in understanding ancient religious traditions. Now, we shift our focus to another crucial lens through which to examine these belief systems: geography. The physical environment, far from being a passive backdrop, actively shaped the development and expression of religious ideas and practices. The impact of geography on religion is multifaceted, ranging from the influence of natural resources and environmental challenges to the facilitation of cultural exchange and the emergence of distinct religious landscapes.

Consider, for example, the role of rivers in the development of ancient civilizations and their religious systems. Mesopotamia, situated between the Tigris and Euphrates rivers, was a land of abundance, but also of vulnerability to floods and droughts. This precarious relationship with the environment profoundly influenced religious beliefs and practices. Deities associated with water, such as Enki (Ea) in Sumerian mythology, held paramount importance. Rituals focused on appeasing these deities to ensure the fertility of the land and the prosperity of the people. The annual flooding of the rivers, while essential for agriculture, also presented a constant threat, leading to the development of complex irrigation systems and a profound sense of dependence on the capricious forces of nature, reflected in the cyclical nature of many Mesopotamian myths and religious festivals.

In contrast, the Egyptian civilization flourished along the Nile River, a more predictable and benevolent waterway than its Mesopotamian counterparts. While floods were still a concern, the Nile provided a relatively stable and reliable source of water, enabling the development of a more settled agricultural society. This stability is reflected in Egyptian religious beliefs, which emphasized order, harmony, and cyclical renewal, mirroring the predictable rhythms of the Nile’s inundation and retreat. The Nile itself was considered sacred, personified as the god Hapi, and its annual flooding was seen as a divinely orchestrated event, sustaining life and renewal. The predictable cycles of the Nile contributed to the Egyptians' emphasis on cyclical time and their elaborate funerary practices, reflecting a belief in the cyclical nature of life and death, mirroring the cyclical nature of the river.

The mountainous terrain of Greece, with its isolated valleys and scattered settlements, contrasted sharply with the riverine civilizations of Mesopotamia and Egypt. The geographic isolation of these communities fostered a diversity of religious beliefs and practices, reflected in the multitude of local deities and cults. The rugged landscape itself became imbued with religious significance, with mountains and caves often associated with divine beings or serving as locations for sacred rituals. This rugged landscape and relative isolation compared to Egypt and Mesopotamia arguably fostered a more diverse array of religious traditions and practices in ancient Greece, with less emphasis on centralized religious authority and more emphasis on localized cults and beliefs. The mythology of Greece, with its numerous gods and goddesses, reflects this decentralized religious structure.

Moving eastward to India, the vast subcontinent’s diverse geography – encompassing towering Himalayas, fertile plains, and arid deserts – profoundly shaped the development of its religious traditions. The Himalayas, for example, became imbued with religious significance, serving as the abode of various deities and inspiring the development of ascetic practices aimed at spiritual transcendence. The Ganges River, similarly to the Nile, held immense religious significance, considered sacred and its waters possessing purifying powers. The diverse ecological zones of India fostered regional variations in religious practices, with certain deities and rituals becoming more prominent in specific geographical regions. The development of Hinduism, Buddhism, and Jainism, with their varied beliefs and practices, can be partially attributed to the geographical diversity of the Indian subcontinent.

The impact of geography extended beyond the physical environment to encompass the interactions between different cultures. The Fertile Crescent, for instance, served as a crossroads of civilizations, facilitating the exchange of religious ideas and practices. The diffusion of religious beliefs across geographical boundaries is evident in the shared motifs, narratives, and rituals found in various ancient Near Eastern religions. The spread of religious ideas could be facilitated by trade routes, migrations, and conquest, resulting in a complex interplay of religious influences. Such interactions often led to the syncretism of different religious traditions, the blending of various beliefs and practices into new and hybrid forms.

The distribution of resources also played a significant role in shaping religious beliefs. Societies with abundant resources often developed more complex and elaborate religious systems, while those with limited resources might have simpler and more pragmatic religious practices. The availability of specific materials, such as certain types of wood or stone, could also influence the design and construction of religious structures and artifacts.

Furthermore, geographical features could act as barriers to cultural exchange, leading to the development of distinct religious traditions in different regions. Mountains, deserts, and oceans could isolate communities, leading to the evolution of unique religious practices and beliefs. The isolation of some communities, while limiting their interaction with other cultures, may have fostered the development of unique religious traditions which were distinct from those found in neighboring regions. Such isolation, paradoxically, could lead to greater cultural and religious homogeneity within the isolated community itself.

In conclusion, geography played a multifaceted role in shaping religious beliefs and practices in the ancient world. Environmental conditions, natural resources, and the interactions between different cultures all contributed to the development of diverse religious landscapes. By considering the geographical context in which religious traditions emerged, we gain a deeper understanding of the complex interplay between the physical environment and human beliefs. The interactions of humans with the natural world have always been fundamental in shaping both the beliefs and practices of the various cultures examined, showcasing how geographical features and cultural interactions shaped the development and dissemination of religious thought and practices. This understanding enhances our interpretation of ancient religious texts and practices, revealing the intricate relationship between human spiritual endeavors and the physical world they inhabited. The study of religion is incomplete without a thorough consideration of its geographical context, recognizing the interplay between location, environment and the beliefs and practices of a civilization.

The Role of Trade Routes in the Spread of Religious Ideas

The preceding discussion established the profound influence of geography on the development of ancient religious traditions. However, the physical landscape was not the sole determinant of religious dissemination. The movement of people and goods along established trade routes played a crucial, and often overlooked, role in the spread of religious ideas and practices across vast distances. These networks of exchange, far from being merely economic arteries, acted as conduits for the transmission of cultural elements, including religious beliefs, rituals, and iconography.

The Silk Road, perhaps the most famous example of an ancient trade route, vividly illustrates this phenomenon. Stretching thousands of miles from East Asia to the Mediterranean, the Silk Road facilitated the exchange of not only silk, spices, and precious goods, but also religious ideas. Buddhism, originating in India, spread significantly along this route, reaching Central Asia, China, and even parts of Southeast Asia. The journey of Buddhist monks and traders along the Silk Road facilitated the establishment of monasteries, the translation of scriptures, and the adaptation of Buddhist teachings to local cultures. The interaction of Buddhism with pre-existing belief systems along the Silk Road led to the development of syncretic religious traditions, blending elements of Buddhism with indigenous faiths. For example, the assimilation of Buddhist concepts into existing Chinese philosophies and practices is evident in the development of Chan (Zen) Buddhism. The interactions between different religious traditions along the Silk Road often led to a mutual exchange and adaptation of beliefs and practices.

Similarly, the maritime trade routes connecting India, Southeast Asia, and China also played a vital role in the spread of religious ideas. Buddhist missionaries and traders traveled by sea, establishing monasteries and spreading Buddhist teachings across the Indian Ocean. The interaction of Buddhism with local traditions led to the emergence of diverse forms of Buddhism in Southeast Asia, each adapted to the specific cultural context. The development of Theravada Buddhism in Southeast Asia is a clear example of this process, demonstrating the adaptability of religious traditions to new environments and the influence of sea trade routes. These maritime trade networks also facilitated the spread of other religious traditions, such as Hinduism and Islam, to various parts of Southeast Asia and beyond. The spread of religious ideas through these routes was not a passive process; it was an active and dynamic one, involving the adaptation and transformation of religious doctrines and practices in response to new cultural contexts.

The Incense Road, another significant trade route in the ancient world, connected the southern Arabian Peninsula with the Mediterranean world. This route facilitated the spread of various religious ideas and practices, including those associated with ancient Semitic religions and later, Christianity. The Incense Road connected various cultures, facilitating exchange of religious beliefs and practices. The spread of Christianity through the Roman Empire, for example, was aided by existing trade routes, which enabled the rapid dissemination of religious messages and the establishment of communities of faith in various regions. The Apostle Paul's journeys can be seen as an example of this, as he utilized established trade networks to spread his teachings and establish churches. The adoption of Christianity in diverse cultural contexts led to the emergence of distinct Christian traditions, which were shaped by their interactions with local cultures and beliefs.

Beyond these well-known trade routes, numerous less prominent but equally significant networks of exchange contributed to the spread of religious ideas. Local and regional trade routes, often connecting smaller settlements and villages, played a vital role in the dissemination of religious beliefs within specific regions. These smaller scale networks facilitated the transmission of religious knowledge, the spread of ritual practices, and the establishment of localized religious communities. The movement of goods and people along these routes created opportunities for the exchange of cultural information, which played a significant role in shaping the development and transmission of religious traditions.

The role of trade routes in the dissemination of religious ideas was not limited to the physical movement of people and goods. The exchange of material culture, such as religious artifacts, scriptures, and iconography, also contributed significantly to the transmission of religious beliefs. The presence of similar religious symbols or artifacts in geographically distant regions often suggests the influence of trade routes in the spread of religious ideas. The trade networks facilitated the circulation of religious texts and images, disseminating religious concepts and practices across wide regions. This exchange was often accompanied by the adaptation and interpretation of religious symbols and ideas to suit local contexts.

Furthermore, the economic benefits derived from trade often created incentives for the adoption of new religious beliefs. The establishment of trade routes facilitated interactions between different communities, which often led to the adoption of religious practices and beliefs that were viewed as economically advantageous. This economic aspect is demonstrated in the spread of various religions along trade routes, where communities adopted beliefs that promised economic benefits, social order, or political stability. The relationship between religion and trade was not simply one of transmission; it often involved a complex negotiation between economic interests and religious beliefs. The adoption of certain religious beliefs or practices in certain regions was influenced by the perceived economic advantages associated with those particular religions.

The influence of trade routes on the spread of religious ideas also varied across different periods and regions. The pace and extent of religious dissemination were frequently determined by the stability and accessibility of trade routes, as well as the political and social circumstances of the time. In times of peace and political stability, trade flourished, and the exchange of religious ideas was facilitated. Conversely, periods of conflict or political instability often disrupted trade networks, hindering the spread of religious beliefs. Trade routes played an important role in religious dissemination, but their influence varied over time and in different geographic regions.

Moreover, the interactions between different religious traditions along trade routes often led to the emergence of syncretic religious practices, combining elements of various belief systems. The blending of indigenous religious traditions with newly introduced religions, facilitated by trade routes, demonstrates the adaptability of religious beliefs and practices to new contexts. The exchange of religious ideas resulted in the adoption of new beliefs and practices, which were assimilated into local traditions, forming hybrid religious forms. These syncretic practices highlight the fluidity and dynamism of religious traditions.

The combination of beliefs from various sources often resulted in more complex religious systems.

In conclusion, trade routes served as crucial pathways for the dissemination of religious ideas in the ancient world. The movement of people and goods along these networks facilitated the exchange of religious beliefs, rituals, and material culture, contributing significantly to the spread of religious traditions across vast distances and various cultures. The interplay between trade and religion was complex and dynamic, shaped by economic considerations, political circumstances, and cultural interactions. Understanding the role of trade routes in the spread of religious ideas provides essential insights into the interconnectedness of ancient civilizations and the multifaceted nature of religious transmission. By studying the connections between trade and religion, we can gain a richer understanding of the global reach of ancient faiths and the cultural exchange that shaped their development and evolution. The legacy of these ancient trade routes is visible in the diverse and syncretic religious landscape of the world today.

Chronological Developments in Religious Traditions

Having explored the geographical influences on the dissemination of ancient religious traditions, we now turn our attention to the chronological development of these faiths. Understanding the historical timeline is crucial to appreciating the evolution of religious beliefs and practices, as well as the interactions between different traditions. The development of each religion was not a static process but a dynamic one, shaped by historical events, social changes, and cultural interactions.

The earliest forms of religious expression often involved animistic beliefs and ancestor veneration, common across numerous ancient societies. These practices, focusing on the spirits inhabiting the natural world and honoring deceased relatives, laid the groundwork for more formalized religious systems. The development of agriculture played a significant role in this evolution. As settled communities emerged, the need for social cohesion and explanations for natural phenomena led to the emergence of more complex religious structures and belief systems. The development of priesthoods and temples further institutionalized religious practices, lending an air of authority and permanence to religious beliefs.

In ancient Mesopotamia, the Sumerian civilization developed a sophisticated pantheon of gods and goddesses, represented in their epic poems and hymns. The Epic of Gilgamesh, arguably one of the earliest surviving works of literature, encapsulates Sumerian cosmology and their understanding of life, death, and the divine. The story reflects a preoccupation with mortality and the search for immortality, themes that resonate across many religious traditions. The development of cuneiform writing allowed for the preservation and dissemination of religious texts, contributing to the continuity of Sumerian religious beliefs for centuries. The subsequent Akkadian, Babylonian, and Assyrian empires inherited and adapted Sumerian religious traditions, incorporating elements into their own belief systems. This process of assimilation and adaptation demonstrates the fluidity of religious traditions and their capacity to evolve in response to cultural changes.

Ancient Egypt witnessed the development of a complex religious system characterized by a vast pantheon of gods and goddesses, elaborate rituals, and an elaborate belief in the afterlife. The Book of the Dead, a collection of spells and prayers intended to guide the deceased through the afterlife, provides invaluable insight into Egyptian religious beliefs and practices. The pharaohs played a central role in Egyptian religion, considered divine intermediaries between the gods and the people. The construction of monumental pyramids and temples served as physical manifestations of their religious beliefs, highlighting the importance of religion in Egyptian society. Egyptian religious beliefs were significantly shaped by the Nile River, which dictated their agricultural cycle and daily life. The cyclical flooding of the Nile was interpreted as a divine act, generating a close relationship between the environment and their spiritual beliefs.

In ancient Greece, the development of polytheism involved a diverse pantheon of gods and goddesses, each associated with specific aspects of nature, human life, or societal functions. Greek mythology, transmitted through epic poetry, plays, and artistic representations, provided a framework for understanding the cosmos and human relationships with the divine. The Olympian gods, dwelling atop Mount Olympus, were the principal deities in the Greek pantheon. Greek religion was deeply integrated into daily life, with numerous festivals and rituals associated with specific gods and events. The oracle at Delphi, renowned for its prophetic pronouncements, held considerable influence, shaping political and personal decisions. The evolution of Greek philosophical thought gradually challenged traditional religious beliefs, culminating in the development of philosophical schools that questioned the nature of divinity and the existence of gods.

In the Roman world, the adoption and adaptation of Greek religious beliefs led to the creation of a syncretic religious tradition. The Romans incorporated many aspects of Greek mythology and religion into their own, associating their gods with their Greek counterparts. The Roman pantheon displayed a similar structure to the Greek pantheon, with similar functions and attributes assigned to their gods. The Roman emperors, like the Egyptian pharaohs, cultivated a close relationship with the divine, asserting their divine authority to maintain order and legitimacy. The Roman Empire's vast geographical reach facilitated the spread of Roman religious practices and beliefs throughout the Mediterranean world, influencing the development of other religious traditions. The rise of Christianity within the Roman Empire eventually led to a profound shift in the religious landscape, resulting in the decline of traditional Roman religious practices.

Buddhism, originating in India with Siddhartha Gautama (the Buddha), spread widely through missionary efforts and trade routes. The early development of Buddhism focused on the Four Noble Truths and the Eightfold Path, aimed at achieving enlightenment and escaping the cycle of suffering. Different schools of Buddhist thought emerged over time, reflecting diverse interpretations and adaptations of the

Buddha's teachings. Theravada Buddhism emphasized monastic life and individual practice, while Mahayana Buddhism expanded on the concept of Bodhisattvas, enlightened beings who delay their own Nirvana to aid others. The spread of Buddhism to Central Asia, East Asia, and Southeast Asia involved significant adaptations to local cultural contexts, resulting in distinct forms of Buddhism in different regions.

Judaism, with its roots in ancient Canaan, developed a monotheistic faith, emphasizing a covenant between God and the chosen people. The Torah, comprising the first five books of the Hebrew Bible, forms the foundational text of Judaism. Judaism profoundly influenced the development of Christianity and Islam. The historical trajectory of Judaism is characterized by periods of persecution and diaspora, leading to adaptations and innovations in religious practice and interpretation. The destruction of the Second Temple in Jerusalem was a pivotal moment, leading to the rise of Rabbinic Judaism and the development of the Talmud, a vast compendium of Jewish law, tradition, and interpretation.

Christianity, emerging from within Judaism in the first century CE, experienced rapid growth across the Roman Empire. The life and teachings of Jesus Christ formed the core of Christian beliefs, emphasizing love, compassion, and salvation through faith. The spread of Christianity was facilitated by the existing Roman road network, missionary activities, and the conversion of Roman emperors. Early Christianity faced persecution, but eventually gained official recognition and became the dominant religion of the Roman Empire. Over time, different branches of Christianity developed, leading to the emergence of Catholicism, Orthodoxy, and Protestantism.

Islam, founded by the prophet Muhammad in the seventh century CE, spread rapidly across the Middle East, North Africa, and beyond. The Quran, Islam's holy book, contains the revelations received by Muhammad, laying out Islamic beliefs and practices. Islam emphasizes the oneness of God (Allah) and the submission to His will. The expansion of the Islamic caliphate fostered the spread of Islam across vast territories, leading to the development of diverse Islamic cultures and interpretations of Islamic teachings. Islamic scholarship played a significant role in preserving and expanding upon ancient knowledge, contributing to the intellectual and scientific advancements in various fields.

These chronological developments demonstrate the dynamic nature of religious traditions, highlighting their evolution through historical events, cultural interactions, and interpretations. The continuous interplay between religious beliefs and social, political, and geographical contexts shaped the diverse landscape of religious practices that exists today. Studying this chronological evolution is vital to understanding the complexity and richness of religious experiences across cultures and time. The similarities and differences between these traditions, even amidst their distinct historical trajectories, illuminate the enduring human quest for meaning and purpose.

Cultural Exchange and Syncretism in Religious Traditions

The preceding sections have established the significant influence of geography and chronology on the development of major religious traditions. However, a complete understanding requires acknowledging the crucial role of cultural exchange and syncretism. These processes, often involving the blending of seemingly disparate belief systems, have profoundly shaped the religious landscapes of various civilizations. It is impossible to examine the evolution of any single ancient religion in isolation; their narratives are intricately interwoven through centuries of interaction and mutual influence. This subsection will delve into specific examples demonstrating the dynamic interplay between cultures and their impact on religious belief and practice.

One of the most striking examples of religious syncretism is found in the Roman Empire. Initially characterized by a relatively tolerant approach towards diverse religious practices within its vast territories, Rome did not initially impose a single state religion. This policy facilitated the influx and integration of various religious traditions. The Romans, known for their pragmatic approach, frequently adopted and adapted foreign deities, integrating them into their own pantheon. Greek gods, with their established myths and narratives, were particularly susceptible to this process of Romanization. Zeus became Jupiter, Hera became Juno, Poseidon became Neptune, and so forth. These weren't merely name changes; Roman artists, poets, and writers reinterpreted these figures, adapting them to Roman values and cultural contexts. This process went beyond simple name substitution; Roman artists often depicted these deities in styles that reflected Roman artistic conventions, further emphasizing the fusion of religious and cultural identities. The resulting Roman pantheon became a fascinating tapestry of assimilated deities, each possessing a unique blend of Greek and Roman attributes and characteristics. This syncretic approach allowed the Roman Empire to maintain a sense of unity amidst its diverse population, while accommodating existing religious beliefs and practices, at least until the rise of Christianity.

The integration of foreign cults into Roman religion was not limited to Greek traditions. Egyptian deities, like Isis, gained significant popularity within the Roman Empire. Isis's cult, characterized by its emphasis on motherhood, healing, and magic, resonated with the Roman populace, transcending cultural boundaries. Similarly, the worship of Mithras, a Persian deity, became widespread among Roman soldiers and civilians. Mithraism, with its elaborate mystery rites and emphasis on initiation and brotherhood, attracted a devoted following. This spread of Mithraism exemplifies the fluidity of religious boundaries during this period. The popularity of these foreign cults served as a testament to the Roman Empire's capacity for religious absorption and adaptation. Moreover, this process of religious exchange was not one-sided; the interaction between Roman and other cultures led to the modification and reinterpretation of these foreign traditions. The Roman adaptation of foreign deities often influenced the very nature of the original cults, further showcasing the transformative power of cultural exchange.

Beyond the Roman Empire, the spread of Buddhism offers compelling evidence of cultural exchange and religious adaptation. Originating in India, Buddhism's journey across Asia involved a significant degree of cultural syncretism. As Buddhism spread to different regions, such as China, Tibet, Japan, and Southeast Asia, its tenets and practices were often adapted to local cultural contexts. In China, for example, Buddhism incorporated elements of Confucianism and Taoism, leading to the development of unique schools of Buddhist thought, such as Chan Buddhism (Zen in Japanese). These syncretic forms of Buddhism demonstrated the capacity of religious traditions to integrate and coexist with existing belief systems, resulting in a blend of doctrines and practices. In Tibet, the integration of Buddhism with indigenous Bon traditions resulted in Tibetan Buddhism, a unique branch characterized by its emphasis on tantric practices and its integration with local spiritual beliefs. The presence of protective deities and local folk beliefs within Tibetan Buddhism, for example, is a direct manifestation of this process of cultural assimilation. Similarly, in Japan, Buddhism interacted with Shinto, leading to the development of unique syncretic forms that blended Buddhist and Shinto practices and beliefs.

The interaction between Judaism, Christianity, and Islam provides another significant case study in cultural exchange and religious adaptation. Christianity emerged from Judaism, inheriting many of its core beliefs and practices. The Hebrew Bible, with its stories and teachings, became the Old Testament of the Christian Bible. However, the emergence of Christianity brought significant transformations in religious practice and interpretation, notably the central role of Jesus Christ and the emphasis on salvation through faith. Islam, in turn, built upon the Abrahamic heritage, incorporating elements from Judaism and Christianity while establishing its unique theological framework. The Quran recognizes both Moses and Jesus as prophets, acknowledging the continuity of religious traditions while establishing the primacy of Muhammad's message. The spread of Islam involved the integration with existing cultural and religious traditions. The Islamic Golden Age, characterized by significant intellectual and scientific advancements, saw the incorporation and expansion upon ancient knowledge, further showcasing the dynamic interplay between religious and intellectual pursuits.

The examples cited above illustrate that cultural exchange and syncretism are not exceptional events, but rather integral processes shaping the development of religious traditions. The interaction between religious traditions was often characterized by both cooperation and conflict; however, the exchange of ideas, beliefs, and practices inevitably led to the evolution of new religious forms. Understanding these interactions necessitates a nuanced approach that recognizes both the diversity and interconnectedness of religious traditions. The process of cultural exchange is not always a harmonious blending; it can be a complex and often contested interaction, involving power dynamics and competition. However, despite the challenges and conflicts, the resulting religious landscape reflects a fascinating tapestry of adaptation, innovation, and the enduring capacity of human societies to integrate diverse belief systems. The seemingly contrasting narratives often share underlying themes, reflecting a fundamental human desire for meaning, purpose, and connection to the divine. The study of these interwoven trajectories offers a richer appreciation for the complexity and beauty of human religious experience. The fluidity and adaptability of religious traditions underscore the ongoing evolution of religious thought and practice in response to changing social, political, and environmental contexts, a dynamic process that continues to unfold in our contemporary world. Recognizing the pervasive influence of cultural exchange and syncretism provides a more complete and nuanced understanding of the development of ancient religious traditions, challenging simplistic notions of isolated religious development and highlighting the enduring interconnectedness of human civilizations.

Geographic and Chronological Factors as Shaping Forces in Religious History

The preceding discussion has highlighted the intricate interplay of cultural exchange and syncretism in shaping the religious landscape of ancient civilizations. However, equally crucial are the geographic and chronological factors that profoundly influenced the trajectory of religious development. These factors, often intertwined with cultural exchange, acted as powerful shaping forces, molding beliefs, practices, and the very structures of religious institutions. To understand the tapestry of ancient religions, we must appreciate the unique contributions of both time and place.

Geography, in its broadest sense, encompasses more than just physical location. It includes climate, topography, access to resources, and the opportunities for interaction with other cultures. Consider, for instance, the impact of river systems. The Nile in Egypt, the Tigris and Euphrates in Mesopotamia, and the Indus in India, provided fertile land for agriculture, supporting dense populations and fostering the development of complex societies. These societies, in turn, generated sophisticated religious systems, often centered around the cyclical rhythms of the rivers and the bounty they provided. The dependence on these lifelines fostered a strong connection to the natural world and a deep reverence for the forces that controlled the ebb and flow of the river, impacting the theological frameworks developed by the respective civilizations. Deities associated with water, fertility, and the harvest held prominent positions in the pantheons of these riverine cultures. The predictability of the annual floods, while beneficial, also instilled a sense of awe and dependence on higher powers, influencing religious beliefs and rituals profoundly.

In contrast, civilizations developing in harsher environments, such as those in mountainous or desert regions, faced different challenges. The scarcity of resources and the unpredictable nature of the environment could lead to different religious perspectives, perhaps emphasizing survival, resilience, and a more austere relationship with the divine. Consider the nomadic cultures of the Arabian Peninsula, where the harsh desert landscape likely shaped religious views centered on survival, resource management, and a strong connection to the natural world. The scarcity of water and the uncertainties of the nomadic life likely contributed to the development of religious beliefs that emphasized resilience, divine provision, and the importance of community and mutual support. These geographic factors were deeply embedded in the theological constructs of the early Arabian religions.

Chronology, the passage of time, also played a significant role in shaping religious traditions. The historical context in which a religion emerged greatly influenced its doctrines, practices, and overall trajectory. For example, the development of early Christianity occurred within the context of the Roman Empire, a factor that significantly affected its spread and evolution. The established infrastructure of the Roman road system facilitated the rapid dissemination of Christian ideas across vast territories. Moreover, the Roman legal system, despite its periods of persecution, eventually provided a framework for the organization of the Christian Church. The Roman emphasis on law, order, and centralized authority left an undeniable imprint on the structure of the early Church.

The chronological proximity of various religious traditions also resulted in instances of both influence and conflict. The spread of Buddhism across Asia demonstrates how chronological factors intersected with geographic ones, impacting the development of diverse religious traditions. The early phases of Buddhism saw the dissemination of its teachings across geographical barriers, often influenced by the prevailing political and cultural climates in different regions. The different interpretations and adaptations reflected the unique social and cultural environments that Buddhism encountered along its geographic journey. Chronologically, the different schools of Buddhism that emerged in Southeast Asia, East Asia, and Tibet reflect this long-term evolution. The timeline of its development influenced the way it engaged with indigenous religious and philosophical traditions in each location, resulting in significant variations in doctrines, practices, and ritual expressions.

Furthermore, the chronological evolution of religious ideas within a specific tradition reveals how beliefs and practices changed over time. Within Judaism, for instance, the period of the Second Temple saw significant developments in religious thought, culminating in the emergence of various schools of interpretation and legal traditions. These schools of thought, such as the Pharisees, Sadducees, and Essenes, influenced the development of subsequent religious traditions like Christianity and Islam. The chronological evolution of Judaism provides a crucial historical backdrop for understanding the development of related Abrahamic religions. The interplay of historical events, social structures, and theological developments over time within Judaism directly shaped the theological foundations of both Christianity and Islam.

Consider also the impact of major historical events on religious development. The destruction of the Second Temple in Jerusalem in 70 CE profoundly impacted Jewish religious practice, leading to the rise of Rabbinic Judaism and the establishment of new forms of religious authority and leadership. This event marked a significant turning point in Jewish history, and the subsequent responses to this catastrophe shaped religious thought and practice within Judaism. The destruction had a ripple effect, influencing the development of related religious traditions that either built upon or reacted against the Jewish heritage, resulting in fundamental shifts in religious practices, interpretations, and theological understanding.

The interplay between geography and chronology is even more evident when examining the spread of Islam. Beginning in the Arabian Peninsula, Islam expanded rapidly across vast territories, encountering diverse cultures and religious traditions. The geographic factors – including trade routes, established empires, and the existing social structures – influenced the pace and pattern of its spread. The chronological sequence of conquests and interactions shaped the development of Islamic culture and religious practice in different regions. The diverse adaptations of Islam in various parts of the world showcase the influence of local customs and beliefs on the integration of the Islamic faith into distinct cultural contexts.

In conclusion, the evolution of religious traditions is not a linear or isolated process. The interplay of geographic and chronological factors, interwoven with cultural exchange and syncretism, has created a rich and complex tapestry of religious beliefs and practices. By carefully considering these shaping forces, we can achieve a more nuanced and comprehensive understanding of the historical development of religions, appreciating the intricate interplay of diverse factors in molding the religious landscape of ancient civilizations. This understanding necessitates moving beyond simplistic narratives of isolated religious development and acknowledging the pervasive influence of geographical location, the passage of time, and the dynamic interaction between cultures, contributing to the enduring richness and complexity of human religious experience. The seemingly disparate traditions often reveal surprising parallels, underscoring the universality of human spiritual quests and the persistent search for meaning and purpose in a complex and ever-changing world.

Synthesizing Key Findings and Common Threads

Having explored the diverse tapestry of ancient religious traditions—from the Mesopotamian flood narratives to the Egyptian Book of the Dead, from the philosophical intricacies of Buddhism to the ethical pronouncements of the Abrahamic faiths—a striking pattern emerges. Despite the vast geographical distances, the chronological gaps, and the seemingly disparate cultural contexts in which these traditions arose, a remarkable convergence of themes and archetypes consistently appears. This is not to suggest a singular origin point or a direct line of influence in every instance; rather, the recurring motifs point to a deeper, perhaps even inherent, human tendency to grapple with fundamental existential questions in surprisingly similar ways.

One of the most pervasive themes across these traditions is the concept of creation. While the specifics vary considerably—from the divine craftsmanship of the Abrahamic God to the cosmic egg of some Eastern traditions, or the primordial chaos from which order emerges in many creation myths—the underlying narrative remains consistent: a transition from a state of primordial void or chaos to a structured, ordered universe. This narrative reflects a fundamental human desire to understand our origins, to place ourselves within a larger cosmic framework, and to find meaning in the existence of the universe itself. The creation narratives often serve as the foundation upon which subsequent theological, ethical, and cosmological frameworks are built. The methods of creation, the nature of the creator(s), and the resulting order frequently reflect the cultural values and societal structures of the civilizations that produced them. Yet, the fundamental act of creation, the transition from nothingness to something, persists as a powerful unifying motif.

Closely linked to creation narratives are stories of deluge and destruction. The Epic of Gilgamesh, the Sumerian flood account, and the biblical flood narrative all share a common thread: a catastrophic event that wipes away existing order, often as punishment for human wickedness or transgression. This catastrophic event is followed by a promise of renewal or rebirth, a new beginning. This cyclical pattern of destruction and renewal underscores the fragility of human civilization and the recurring theme of judgment and redemption. It speaks to a fundamental human fear of annihilation and a simultaneous hope for resurgence, a resilience inherent in the human spirit. The specific details of these cataclysms and the mechanisms of divine judgment vary significantly across the narratives, yet the underlying motif of destruction followed by renewal remains remarkably persistent. The differing accounts reflect the distinct societal anxieties and cultural perspectives of the respective civilizations, yet they all grapple with similar questions of divine justice, human fallibility, and the cyclical nature of existence.

Another recurring motif is the concept of a divine or transcendent power. While the nature and attributes of this power vary widely—from the pantheon of gods in ancient Greece and Rome to the monotheistic God of Judaism, Christianity, and Islam—the idea of a force or being beyond the material world that exerts influence on human affairs is a common thread. This transcendent power often takes on anthropomorphic qualities, mirroring human emotions and motivations, yet simultaneously possesses characteristics surpassing human comprehension. The varying conceptions of the divine reflect the complex interplay of cultural beliefs, societal structures, and philosophical thought. However, the fundamental notion of a superior force, often responsible for creation and ultimate judgment, appears consistently across these diverse traditions, highlighting the universality of the human need to seek a source of ultimate authority and meaning beyond the limitations of the earthly realm. The varying attributes assigned to the deity often provide a lens through which to examine the specific concerns and hopes of the respective cultures.

Furthermore, the concept of morality and ethical codes emerges consistently. The Ten Commandments, the Buddhist Eightfold Path, and the various ethical prescriptions found in ancient Egyptian texts and Greek philosophy all emphasize the importance of ethical conduct. While the specific rules and principles differ, the underlying message remains remarkably consistent: human actions have consequences, and adherence to a moral code is essential for individual and societal well-being. This suggests an innate human sense of morality, a universal understanding of the importance of ethical behaviour for the smooth functioning of society and the pursuit of a fulfilling existence. The varying formulations of these ethical codes reflect the evolution of moral thought and the development of different social structures. However, the fundamental belief in the importance of morality and the pursuit of righteous conduct remains a remarkable commonality across diverse traditions.

The archetypal figures—heroes, villains, divine messengers, and wise teachers—further illustrate the remarkable similarities across diverse ancient religious traditions. Figures like Gilgamesh, Moses, Buddha, and Krishna, though operating within distinct cultural and historical settings, exemplify human struggles, triumphs, and spiritual quests. These figures, regardless of their specific actions and motivations, serve as vehicles for exploring fundamental human experiences and conveying enduring moral lessons.

Their journeys often involve trials, temptations, and eventual enlightenment or redemption, mirroring the universal human experience of striving for meaning and purpose. The varied interpretations and appropriations of these archetypal figures underscore the adaptable nature of myths and the power of these narratives to resonate across time and cultures. Their enduring presence in religious traditions speaks to the universality of human experiences and the enduring power of storytelling to convey profound truths about the human condition.

In conclusion, the comparative analysis of these ancient religious traditions reveals not simply a collection of disparate beliefs and practices but a complex interplay of recurring themes and archetypes. The concepts of creation, destruction and renewal, transcendent power, morality, and archetypal figures consistently appear, underscoring the surprising convergence of human spiritual aspirations across cultures and time. This convergence suggests that these narratives are not simply arbitrary inventions but reflect fundamental aspects of the human condition—our desire to understand our origins, grapple with mortality, find meaning and purpose, and build ethical frameworks for social cohesion. The differences in expression and emphasis are, of course, significant and provide valuable insights into the unique cultural contexts in which these traditions arose. However, the common threads provide a profound testament to the universality of human experience and the enduring human search for meaning and purpose in a complex and often unpredictable world. The study of ancient religions, therefore, offers not only historical understanding but also a unique perspective on the persistent human quest for spiritual truth and ethical guidance. The insights gained can provide valuable context for understanding contemporary religious and ethical dilemmas, underscoring the timeless relevance of these ancient narratives and the continuing search for meaning in the human experience. The enduring power of these narratives lies in their ability to resonate with fundamental human questions, transcending the boundaries of time and culture.

The Enduring Search for Meaning and Purpose

The enduring human search for meaning and purpose is a quest as old as humanity itself. Ancient religious traditions, with their elaborate mythologies, intricate rituals, and codified ethical systems, offer compelling insights into this fundamental aspect of the human condition. While the specific answers vary dramatically across cultures and time periods, the underlying question – what is the meaning of life, and how can we best live it? – remains remarkably consistent. The narratives we've examined, from the Epic of Gilgamesh's desperate pursuit of immortality to the Buddha's path to enlightenment, reflect this universal struggle to find our place in the cosmos and to understand our purpose within a larger framework.

One crucial aspect of this search is the attempt to define our relationship with the transcendent. The diverse conceptions of deity across these traditions—from the polytheistic pantheons of ancient Greece and Rome to the monotheistic God of Judaism, Christianity, and Islam—reveal a deep-seated human need to connect with something greater than ourselves. This connection provides not only a sense of comfort and security but also a framework for understanding the world and our place within it. Even the less overtly theistic traditions, like certain schools of Buddhism, grapple with the concept of ultimate reality and our relationship to it, albeit often within a framework devoid of a personal God. The variations in these theological frameworks are profoundly insightful, offering glimpses into the diverse cultural and historical contexts that shaped these beliefs. The focus on creation myths, for example, reveals societies' anxieties regarding their origins and the nature of the universe, projecting onto their deities the values and concerns that shaped their daily lives.

Beyond the question of the divine, the search for meaning often involves grappling with the concepts of morality and ethics. The ethical codes embedded within these traditions, from the Ten Commandments to the Buddhist Eightfold Path, are not merely arbitrary sets of rules but rather reflections of deeply held societal values and aspirations. These codes aim to define acceptable behavior, promote social cohesion, and provide guidance for navigating the complexities of human interaction. The development and evolution of these ethical frameworks reveal a continuous process of moral reflection and adaptation, shaped by changing social circumstances and evolving understandings of the human condition. The comparisons reveal common ground, such as the near-universal condemnation of violence and theft, yet also illuminate culturally-specific differences, such as varying attitudes towards property or the role of women in society.

The role of ritual and practice in the search for meaning should not be underestimated. Religious rituals, from the elaborate ceremonies of ancient Egypt to the meditative practices of Buddhism, provide a structured framework for engaging with the sacred, reinforcing beliefs, and fostering a sense of community. These practices offer a means of connecting with the transcendent, expressing devotion, and finding solace in times of difficulty. The repetition of prayers, chants, or other ritualistic actions can create a sense of order and stability in a world that often seems chaotic and unpredictable. Moreover, participation in communal rituals fosters a sense of belonging and shared identity, strengthening social bonds and providing support systems within the community. The study of ancient rituals allows us to understand not only the theological beliefs of a particular culture but also their social structures, power dynamics, and psychological needs.

The archetypal figures that populate these ancient narratives —heroes, villains, saviors, and tricksters—offer further insights into the human search for meaning. These figures, often endowed with extraordinary abilities or possessing profound wisdom, serve as models of behavior, embodying ideals and providing inspiration for ethical living. Their stories, though often fantastical, reflect fundamental human experiences: the struggle against adversity, the pursuit of knowledge, the temptations of power, and the search for redemption. The recurrence of similar archetypes across vastly different cultures suggests that these narratives tap into universal aspects of the human psyche, reflecting shared concerns and aspirations. Studying these archetypes allows us to identify the underlying psychological and spiritual needs that these stories address, providing a richer understanding of the enduring power of myths and their continuing relevance in contemporary society.

The cyclical patterns of creation and destruction present in many ancient cosmologies also shed light on the human struggle with mortality and the impermanence of all things. The narratives of floods, cataclysms, and cosmic renewals reflect the fundamental human experience of confronting both our own mortality and the transience of the world around us. These narratives often serve as frameworks for understanding suffering, loss, and the inevitability of change. They also offer hope for renewal and rebirth, highlighting the resilience of the human spirit and the possibility of overcoming adversity. The specific variations in these narratives – whether emphasizing divine punishment, cosmic cycles, or natural disaster – provide crucial insights into the anxieties and worldview of the societies that generated them.

Furthermore, the narratives of divine judgment and redemption reflect a deep-seated human need for justice and accountability. The concept of karma in Buddhism, the Day of Judgment in Abrahamic religions, and the various forms of divine retribution found in ancient mythologies all grapple with the question of moral responsibility and the consequences of our actions. These narratives offer both warnings and promises, highlighting the importance of ethical behavior and providing solace in the face of suffering. The understanding of justice, however, varies significantly across cultures, reflecting differing cultural values and ethical frameworks.

In conclusion, the study of ancient religious traditions provides a profound and multifaceted perspective on the enduring human search for meaning and purpose. These traditions, though diverse in their specific expressions, reflect shared concerns about our origins, our place in the cosmos, our relationships with others, and our ultimate destiny. By examining these ancient narratives, we gain valuable insights not only into the history of religious thought but also into the fundamental aspects of the human condition, revealing the persistent human quest for spiritual truth, ethical guidance, and a sense of purpose in a world often marked by uncertainty and suffering. The enduring relevance of these ancient traditions lies in their continued capacity to resonate with our fundamental questions about life, death, and the meaning of existence. The similarities in their approaches to these questions offer a powerful testament to the universality of the human experience and the enduring power of storytelling to explore these timeless themes. The exploration of these ancient narratives not only illuminates our past but also offers invaluable tools for navigating the complexities of the present and future. The search for meaning, a journey undertaken by countless generations, continues to shape our understanding of ourselves, our world, and our place within the universe.

The Relevance of Ancient Wisdom for Contemporary Society

The exploration of ancient religious traditions reveals a wealth of ethical frameworks and spiritual insights that retain remarkable relevance for contemporary society. While the specific contexts and cultural expressions differ vastly, the underlying concerns with morality, meaning, and the human condition remain strikingly consistent. The enduring value of these ancient wisdom traditions lies not in their literal adherence but in their capacity to offer profound perspectives on the challenges and opportunities of the modern world.

One striking parallel lies in the persistent emphasis on ethical behavior. The ancient codes of conduct, whether the Ten Commandments, the Buddhist Eightfold Path, or the Confucian emphasis on filial piety, all underscore the importance of compassion, justice, and responsible action. These principles, though articulated within specific religious frameworks, resonate deeply with contemporary concerns about social justice, environmental responsibility, and ethical conduct in all aspects of life. The persistent human struggle with issues like inequality, violence, and environmental degradation highlights the continued need for ethical frameworks that guide our actions and promote a more just and sustainable world. The ancient traditions, with their emphasis on empathy and community responsibility, provide a moral compass that remains surprisingly relevant in a rapidly changing world.

The focus on self-awareness and inner transformation found in many ancient traditions also offers valuable tools for navigating the complexities of modern life. Practices like mindfulness meditation, originating in Buddhist traditions, have gained widespread popularity as a means of managing stress, improving focus, and fostering emotional well-being. Similarly, the ancient Greek emphasis on self-knowledge, as exemplified by the Delphic maxim "Know thyself," continues to resonate with contemporary psychology's focus on self-reflection and personal growth. These practices offer pathways to greater emotional intelligence, self-regulation, and a more fulfilling life, countering the pervasive pressures and anxieties of the modern world. The integration of these ancient practices into contemporary therapeutic and wellness approaches demonstrates their ongoing relevance and effectiveness.

Furthermore, the ancient narratives offer valuable insights into the human experience of suffering, loss, and mortality. The Epic of Gilgamesh, for example, grapples with the inevitability of death and the human quest for immortality, a theme that continues to resonate deeply with contemporary anxieties about aging, illness, and the ephemeral nature of life. The diverse ways in which ancient traditions approach the concept of mortality—through reincarnation, afterlife beliefs, or the acceptance of impermanence—provide a rich tapestry of perspectives that can help individuals navigate the challenges of life's inevitable transitions. These ancient frameworks provide a variety of coping mechanisms and philosophical lenses through which to interpret the hardships of life, fostering resilience and acceptance in the face of adversity.

The study of ancient creation myths also offers a different, yet profoundly relevant, perspective. These narratives, though often fantastical, reflect profound questions about origins, purpose, and the relationship between humanity and the cosmos. In a world grappling with the complexities of climate change and ecological crises, the ancient emphasis on the interconnectedness of all things offers a valuable counterpoint to anthropocentric worldviews. The understanding that humanity is but a part of a larger ecological system, as emphasized in many indigenous traditions, challenges the unsustainable practices that threaten the planet's well-being. Reconnecting with the ancient perspective of humanity as an integral part of nature can inspire a more responsible and sustainable approach to environmental stewardship.

Moreover, the ancient emphasis on community and social cohesion offers valuable lessons for contemporary society. The intricate social structures and communal rituals found in ancient cultures highlight the importance of social bonds, mutual support, and shared identity in fostering a thriving society. In an increasingly fragmented and individualistic world, the wisdom traditions emphasize the need for collective action, empathy, and a sense of shared purpose. The ancient examples of communal living, mutual aid, and social responsibility remind us of the essential role of community in promoting well-being and social justice. The rise of community-based initiatives, social movements, and collaborative efforts highlights the continued relevance of these ancient principles.

However, it's crucial to acknowledge the limitations and potential pitfalls of applying ancient wisdom to contemporary contexts. Many ancient traditions contain elements that are incompatible with modern values, such as patriarchal structures, discriminatory practices, or justifications for violence. A critical and nuanced approach is essential, separating valuable ethical principles from outdated or harmful beliefs and practices. The task lies in discerning the enduring wisdom from the culturally specific or problematic aspects, adapting the relevant insights to the needs and values of contemporary society. This requires a careful and critical engagement with the sources, avoiding uncritical appropriation or the selective adoption of only those elements that support pre-existing beliefs.

In conclusion, the relevance of ancient wisdom for contemporary society lies in its capacity to offer profound insights into the enduring human concerns of morality, meaning, and the search for purpose. The ethical principles, spiritual practices, and philosophical perspectives derived from ancient religious traditions provide valuable tools for navigating the challenges and opportunities of the modern world. By critically engaging with these traditions, we can access timeless wisdom that enhances our understanding of ourselves, our relationships with each other, and our place in the larger cosmos. This critical engagement demands a careful consideration of historical context, a sensitivity to diversity, and a commitment to adapting ancient insights to the specific needs and challenges of the present day. The ongoing dialogue between ancient wisdom and contemporary concerns promises to yield rich insights and contribute to a more ethical, compassionate, and sustainable future. The journey of understanding ourselves and our place in the world is a continuous process, and the wisdom traditions offer a rich and diverse resource for navigating this journey. The power of these ancient narratives lies not only in their historical significance but also in their capacity to illuminate the enduring human quest for meaning, purpose, and a more just and fulfilling life. The ongoing relevance of these traditions is a testament to the enduring nature of the human condition and the timeless search for wisdom and understanding. By engaging thoughtfully with these ancient texts and traditions, we can unearth powerful tools and perspectives to address the challenges of our time and build a better future.

Future Directions in Comparative Religious Studies

The preceding chapters have illuminated the remarkable parallels and surprising convergences found across a range of ancient religious traditions. We've seen how seemingly disparate belief systems, born in geographically and chronologically distinct contexts, share fundamental concerns with morality, meaning-making, and the human condition. However, the exploration of ancient wisdom traditions doesn't end with the identification of these shared themes. Instead, it opens up a rich tapestry of avenues for future research and innovative methodologies within the field of comparative religious studies.

One critical area for future inquiry is the expansion of the scope of comparative analysis beyond the traditions already examined. While the focus on ancient Greek, Roman, Egyptian, Buddhist, and Abrahamic faiths provides a robust foundation, incorporating other significant belief systems will further enrich our understanding of human spirituality. Indigenous belief systems, for example, offer invaluable perspectives on the relationship between humanity and nature, often emphasizing ecological interconnectedness and sustainable practices. A more inclusive approach would incorporate the rich diversity of shamanistic traditions, animist beliefs, and the wisdom of indigenous communities worldwide. Examining these traditions, often marginalized in mainstream scholarship, can reveal previously unexplored dimensions of human religious experience and significantly broaden the scope of comparative studies. A comparative framework that actively seeks to decolonize and decentralize the existing academic canons will yield a far richer and more nuanced understanding of human religious expression across cultures and throughout history.

Furthermore, the application of interdisciplinary methodologies holds immense promise for enhancing the rigor and insights of comparative religious studies. The incorporation of insights from anthropology, sociology, psychology, cognitive science, and even neuroscience can provide a more comprehensive understanding of religious phenomena. Anthropological perspectives, for instance, can illuminate the social functions of religious practices and beliefs within specific cultural contexts. Sociological analysis can reveal the ways in which religious institutions shape social structures and power dynamics. Psychological studies can explore the individual motivations and experiences associated with religious faith. By integrating these diverse disciplinary perspectives, researchers can construct a more holistic and nuanced picture of the complex interplay between religious belief, cultural practices, and individual experience. In this vein, exploring the neurobiological underpinnings of religious experience – investigating the brain mechanisms associated with spiritual practices like meditation or prayer – can contribute to a deeper understanding of the neurological aspects of spirituality.

The development of innovative digital methodologies also presents significant opportunities for advancing comparative religious studies. The digitization of vast collections of ancient texts, archaeological findings, and ethnographic data allows researchers to employ sophisticated computational tools for analysis. Text mining, network analysis, and machine learning techniques can uncover hidden patterns and connections within and across diverse religious traditions. These tools can be applied to identify recurring motifs, themes, and narrative structures in ancient texts, enabling a deeper understanding of how these themes evolved and spread across geographical regions. The ability to conduct large-scale comparative analyses of textual and archaeological data will facilitate the identification of patterns and connections that might otherwise remain hidden to traditional methods of scholarship. The use of digital tools also opens up exciting possibilities for collaborative research projects, allowing scholars across geographical locations to work together on large-scale comparative studies. This interconnectivity is particularly valuable in cross-cultural research that requires the input and expertise from scholars across the world.

Another promising avenue for future research lies in the exploration of the evolutionary dimensions of religious belief. Drawing upon insights from evolutionary biology and cognitive science, scholars can investigate the adaptive functions of religious beliefs and practices. This area requires careful consideration of the potential biases involved, ensuring a robust and ethically responsible approach that doesn't lead to overly simplistic reductionist explanations of religious experiences. Analyzing the evolutionary basis of religious behavior might reveal how certain religious practices and beliefs provided survival advantages for early humans, offering insights into the origins and persistence of religious phenomena across generations. This approach, however, should be pursued with caution and intellectual rigor, avoiding deterministic conclusions and acknowledging the multifaceted nature of human religious experience. Acknowledging the impact of cultural transmission and the influence of social and environmental factors on the development of religious beliefs is essential for providing a balanced and insightful analysis of the evolution of religious practices and belief systems.

Furthermore, the future of comparative religious studies requires a greater emphasis on ethical considerations. As researchers engage with sensitive religious traditions and potentially controversial materials, a commitment to ethical research practices is paramount. This includes obtaining informed consent from communities involved in the research, ensuring respectful representation of diverse perspectives, and acknowledging the potential power imbalances inherent in the study of marginalized traditions. The ethical treatment of data, sensitive information, and the preservation of community knowledge are not just moral imperatives but are also crucial for fostering trust and facilitating productive collaborations with the communities being studied. Moreover, researchers must critically examine their own biases and assumptions, acknowledging the potential influence of their own cultural and religious backgrounds on their interpretations.

In conclusion, the future of comparative religious studies is bright, brimming with exciting opportunities for innovative research and interdisciplinary collaboration. By expanding the scope of analysis, integrating diverse methodologies, embracing digital tools, exploring evolutionary perspectives, and prioritizing ethical considerations, researchers can continue to uncover profound insights into the shared human quest for meaning, purpose, and understanding. The study of ancient religious traditions offers a powerful lens through which to examine the fundamental aspects of the human condition, and the continued exploration of these traditions holds immense promise for enriching our understanding of ourselves and our place in the world. The ongoing dialogue between ancient wisdom and contemporary concerns will yield not only deeper intellectual understanding but also potentially contribute to a more just, compassionate, and sustainable future. The journey of studying comparative religion is a continuing process, one that is enriched by rigorous scholarship, interdisciplinary perspectives, and a commitment to ethical practices. This ongoing endeavor will not only illuminate the past but also shed light on the ongoing human quest for meaning and understanding, a quest as relevant today as it was millennia ago. The challenges and rewards of such an endeavor are substantial, underscoring the necessity of collaborative efforts and a commitment to understanding human experience across cultures and through time. This careful and responsible approach to research will contribute to the creation of a more nuanced and inclusive understanding of the global tapestry of religious belief and practice. Only by engaging with these rich traditions in a mindful, respectful, and ethically sound manner can we fully appreciate their enduring lessons and their ongoing relevance to the contemporary world.

Concluding Reflections on the Universality of Human Spiritual Experiences

The preceding exploration of ancient religious traditions has revealed a remarkable consistency in their underlying concerns and approaches to the fundamental questions of human existence. While the specific narratives, rituals, and deities may vary dramatically across cultures and millennia, a deeper examination unveils a shared human yearning for meaning, purpose, and connection with something transcending the immediate, tangible world. This underlying universality transcends the superficial differences in iconography and mythology, pointing towards a fundamental aspect of the human condition: our inherent spiritual nature.

This inherent spiritual drive manifests in myriad ways. The Epic of Gilgamesh, for instance, with its epic quest for immortality, reflects a deeply ingrained human desire to overcome the limitations of mortality and achieve a sense of lasting significance. This same yearning is echoed in the Egyptian Book of the Dead, where elaborate rituals and spells aimed to ensure a successful transition to the afterlife. Similarly, the Abrahamic traditions, with their emphasis on covenant and divine grace, offer pathways to a transcendent reality and a sense of belonging within a larger cosmic order. Even the seemingly disparate philosophies of ancient Greece, with their focus on reason and virtue, grapple with fundamental questions of existence, purpose, and the nature of reality, ultimately striving for a state of eudaimonia – flourishing or human well-being – often viewed as a spiritual achievement.

The universality of spiritual experience is not limited to the narratives and beliefs systems themselves. The practices associated with these traditions – prayer, meditation, ritual sacrifice, pilgrimage – reveal a common human desire to engage with the sacred, to connect with something beyond the everyday. These practices, while diverse in their forms, all share a common aim: to foster a sense of connection, peace, and meaning. The physical acts of these practices serve to deepen the spiritual experience, often involving bodily movement, voice, and sensory engagement, which enhances the connection to the sacred. The repetitive nature of many spiritual practices, such as chanting or prayer, can induce altered states of consciousness, which further amplify the experience. The collective aspect of many spiritual rituals also underlines the human need for community and shared experience, reinforcing bonds and creating a sense of belonging that transcends the individual.

Moreover, the moral codes embedded within ancient religious traditions, despite their variations, reveal a shared concern with ethical conduct and social harmony. The Ten Commandments, the Buddhist precepts, and the Egyptian concept of Ma'at (truth, justice, and cosmic order) all emphasize the importance of justice, compassion, and responsible behavior. These moral frameworks provide guidelines for navigating social relationships and living a meaningful life, reflecting a fundamental human need for order, predictability, and a sense of purpose within a larger societal context. The emphasis on ethical conduct in these systems underscores the interconnectedness between spiritual and social dimensions of life, reflecting the idea that one cannot truly experience spiritual fulfillment without acting ethically and responsibly towards others. These moral codes are not simply arbitrary rules but rather reflect deeply held intuitions about the importance of cooperation, empathy, and respect for others.

The striking similarities between ancient religious traditions suggest that the human spiritual experience may be, at least in part, rooted in our biology and cognitive architecture. While this is a complex and ongoing area of research, cognitive science and evolutionary psychology offer intriguing insights into the potential neural and psychological underpinnings of religious belief and practice. The human brain's capacity for symbolic thought, abstract reasoning, and the creation of narratives may be key factors in our ability to develop and sustain complex religious systems. The innate human tendency towards pattern recognition, the search for causal explanations, and the desire for meaning and purpose may all contribute to the development of religious belief. Further research into the neurobiological aspects of spiritual experiences, such as prayer, meditation, and ritual, may shed additional light on the underlying mechanisms involved. It's crucial to approach these biological and cognitive investigations with caution, emphasizing that they do not invalidate or diminish the subjective and profound nature of spiritual experiences.

However, it’s crucial to avoid a reductive approach that reduces the richness and complexity of human spirituality to purely biological or psychological factors. The human experience is shaped by a complex interplay of biological predispositions, cultural influences, and individual choices. Religious belief and practice are deeply embedded within social and cultural contexts, with meaning and significance often derived from shared rituals, narratives, and community bonds. The social and cultural dimensions of religious experiences should be acknowledged as equally important as the biological and cognitive factors.

The enduring power of ancient religious traditions lies not only in their historical significance but also in their ongoing relevance to contemporary human experience. Despite advancements in science and technology, fundamental human questions about meaning, purpose, and the nature of reality remain. The ancient wisdom traditions, with their insights into the human condition, offer resources and frameworks for addressing these enduring concerns. Their narratives, rituals, and moral codes provide a rich tapestry of perspectives for navigating life's challenges, fostering personal growth, and connecting with something larger than oneself. The lessons learned from these ancient texts resonate powerfully today, offering wisdom for living an ethical and meaningful life in an increasingly complex world. These traditions highlight the interconnectedness of all life, the importance of compassion and justice, and the profound impact that our actions have on others and the environment.

Furthermore, the study of ancient religious traditions can foster intercultural understanding and dialogue. By acknowledging the shared spiritual aspirations of diverse cultures, we can build bridges of understanding and cultivate a more harmonious and inclusive world. The examination of common themes and archetypes across various faiths can help to overcome prejudices and promote tolerance and respect. This approach recognizes the shared human capacity for spirituality and ethical behavior, highlighting our common humanity rather than our differences. Comparative religious studies, therefore, serves not only as an academic pursuit but also as a vital tool for fostering intercultural dialogue and promoting peace and understanding in an increasingly interconnected world.

In conclusion, the universality of human spiritual experiences, as revealed through the comparative study of ancient religious traditions, points to a fundamental human need for meaning, purpose, and connection. The yearning for something beyond the material world is a recurring theme throughout human history and across cultures, manifesting in diverse narratives, rituals, and ethical frameworks. This inherent spiritual drive, while expressed through varying cultural lenses, underscores a shared human quest for understanding our place in the universe and finding meaning in our lives. This quest is an ongoing journey, and the wisdom found in ancient religious traditions continues to provide invaluable guidance and inspiration for navigating the complexities of contemporary existence. The ongoing engagement with these ancient wisdom traditions promises to be both intellectually stimulating and spiritually enriching, enriching not only our individual lives but also contributing to the creation of a more just, compassionate, and sustainable world. The future of the study of comparative religion lies in the continued, ethical, and responsible exploration of these enduring themes.

Acknowledgments

This book would not have been possible without the generous support and guidance of numerous individuals. We are deeply indebted to many, whose insightful comments and unwavering encouragement were invaluable throughout the research and writing process. The expertise in comparative mythology and ancient history provided crucial direction and helped to shape the central arguments of this work. We also wish to express our sincere gratitude to numerous libraries, and websites, for their assistance in locating and accessing obscure texts and manuscripts. Their dedication and expertise were instrumental in ensuring the comprehensiveness of my research. Furthermore, I am grateful to my colleagues at for their stimulating discussions and feedback, which significantly enhanced the clarity and precision of my analysis. Finally, my heartfelt thanks go to my family and friends for their patience, understanding, and unwavering support during the often challenging process of bringing this project to fruition.

Appendix

Appendix A contains a chronological timeline of the major religious traditions discussed in this book, highlighting key events and developments. Appendix B provides a detailed comparison of the creation myths found in various ancient cultures, outlining their similarities and differences. Appendix C offers a selection of translated excerpts from lesser-known texts referenced throughout the book, providing a deeper glimpse into their specific theological and philosophical concepts.

Glossary

Ma'at: (Ancient Egyptian) The concept of truth, justice, cosmic order, and balance.
Eudaimonia: (Ancient Greek) Flourishing or human well-being; often considered a spiritual achievement.
Kybalion: A hermetic philosophical text outlining seven principles. Specific principles would be defined here as needed.

References

References are included in the pages of this book, in completion with all cited works, formatted according to their specific citation style.

ie. Smith, John. The Epic of Gilgamesh. Oxford University Press, 2000.
Jones, Mary. Ancient Egyptian Religion. Cambridge University Press, 1995.
Brown, David. The Ten Commandments and their Cultural Impact. Routledge, 2010.

Author Biography

About the Authors:

Samantha and Craig McManus are a dynamic husband and wife team specializing in holistic health and wellness. With certifications in hypnotherapy, master healing, spiritual coaching, and more, they bring a wealth of knowledge and passion to their work. Together, they are the proud parents of a family of five, including three spirited children, two daughters and son. Their family journey has been a source of inspiration, fueling their commitment to helping others.

The McManus family believes in the power of personal growth and spiritual exploration. With this book, Samantha and Craig hope to guide others on their spiritual paths, offering tools and insights to help individuals find their own voices and embrace their unique journeys. They aim to create a supportive community where people can connect, share, and grow together in their quest for spiritual fulfillment.

Made in the USA
Columbia, SC
29 April 2025

b98abcc3-50f8-431d-b312-4ff26b497b8dR01